W9-CSY-315

REAL ESTATE UNLEASHED

The game has changed! Do you know how to win it?

Carole Rodoni and Shashank Shekhar

Copyright © 2011 Shashank Shekhar and Carole Rodoni. Except as permitted under the United States copyright act of 1976, no part of this publication may be reproduced or distributed in any form or by any means, or stored in a database or retrieval system, without the prior written permission of the authors.

The publication is designed for accurate and authoritative information in regard to the subject matter covered. It is sold with the understanding that the authors are not engaged in rendering legal, accounting or other professional service. If legal advice or other expert assistance is required, the services of a competent professional person should be sought.

This book is dedicated to all Real Estate Professionals who are committed to a long and rewarding real estate career.

INTRODUCTION

You're a good soldier
Choosing your battles
Pick yourself up
And dust yourself off
Get back in the saddle
You're on the front line
Everyone's watching
You know it's serious
We're getting closer
This isn't over

Shakira, Waka Waka - FIFA World Cup 2010 Official Song

Last few years, the real estate market has gone through very challenging times. So we won't blame you if you are feeling overwhelmed or even anxious. But what's happening to you today has happened before and without doubt would happen again. That's the way this industry behaves.

In our several years of managing businesses, teams and training real estate professionals, we realized that too many people don't get the bigger picture. They are so immersed in what's happening on a daily or a weekly basis that they fail to plan for what's ahead. This book (probably the only one of its kind) tries to rectify that problem.

The real estate industry is unique in a way that it gets impacted by a lot of stuff that happens *outside* the industry for example how is the country's demographics changing or what is going to be the unemployment rate next year.

The book starts by giving you the fundamentals of Economy, Real Estate and Lending. We then delve into some of the major changes that are going to impact the industry in a BIG way. But we don't leave you hanging at that. We provide step-by-step instructions on how you can win this game, the rules of which has been completely changed.

Before, we sign off we would like to thank Steve Borelli for designing the cover of this book and Rajat Grover for spending numerous hours to research for the book.

If you need to get in touch with us for Media interviews, Speaking or Consulting opportunities, hit the "contact us" button on www.RealEstateUnleashedBook.com.

To your success in this incredible journey called Real Estate!

Shashank and Carole

CONTENTS

GET THE BIG PICTURE

You can't know how to increase your business unless you understand the big picture—the economy and how it works, the consumer and how they behave and to grasp how the markets and society all inter-relate and affect each other.

1999 is the year to start to look at the economy because it was the year everyone said was the start of the new economy. But the truth is there never was a "new economy". The old economy was still there—the 90s were just the fifth cycle of the old economy. Economies are like eco systems—they go through cycles and waves, they develop, blossom, wind down and then hibernate until the next rush. These cycles usually last about 50 years—25 years for the build up and then 25 years for the transition, downturn and build up again for the next cycle.

The first boom cycle in the United States began in 1789 in the midst of the Industrial Revolution, which brought people off the farms and into the cities. It lasted for 26 years and was brought to an end by the Napoleonic Wars and the transition/downturn lasted 20 years. The second boom cycle, the Railroad Era, began in 1848. It lasted 25 years and ended in 1872 when 300 railroad companies went bankrupt leaving only a few strong players. The third boom cycle, known as the Belle Époque, began in the late 1800s and lasted 24 years until 1921. It was most say like the 90s because of all the inventions and creativity. It was the time when cars, the telephone and electricity premiered and was one of the greatest periods of wealth creation ever known. The fourth boom cycle, known as the post WWII expansion, began in 1948. It was fuelled by the growth and development of the American economy, the Marshall Plan that rebuilt Europe after the war and the drive for colonial independence in emerging countries around the world. It lasted 26 years until 1974 and was brought to an end by the OPEC oil crisis. The transition/downturn lasted 20 years from 1974 through 1993. The fifth boom cycle, ours, started in the mid 1990s and is being fuelled by new technologies in communication, energy and globalization. The transition started in the late 2000's and the transition/downturn will last another 20 years.

Knowing now that there never was a new economy we can understand more about what has happened during this decade in the economy.

In 2000, after a very prosperous and wild ride in the mid to late 1990s, companies like Enron and Global Crossings began to totter. Inventories began to build up so companies began to finance themselves becoming not only the producer but also the banker. We had a Presidential election that brought government to a stand still for 8 weeks. The young 20-30 year olds who were in charge of many of these new companies thought they knew it all—build it fast, get sales at any price, don't worry about costs and take as much as you can for yourself. Startups were springboards for going public ASAP and no one was thinking about building world-class companies over time.

In 2001 reality hit and people realized that we were in a recession. Both the stock market and the real estate market went in the doldrums and just as the economy was rebounding, September 11th happened and everything stopped once again. The Feds started to bring down interest rates and the government went on a spending spree to help stimulate the economy. The Feds kept lowering interest rate to help ebb the slide. The government was encouraging home ownership and pushing banks to lower the underwriting standards for mortgages so people could qualify. Suddenly real estate became the most sought after of assets and everyone wanted to get into the real estate business.

By 2003 everything was in place to keep the economy moving. Interest rates were at 1 percent, the government continued to spend money like a drunken sailor, inflation was tame at below 3 per cent, unemployment was not a problem at 6.5 percent and our gross domestic product was growing at 4-5 percent. Real estate was on a tear with appreciation in some areas of 20-25 percent. The stock market was positive too. People were feeling wealthy and spending like crazy. Everyone felt we had found the "new economy".

By 2005 the economy was beginning to unwind but no one saw it coming.

In real estate, sales were already declining, inflation was increasing, the stock market was still positive but returns were smaller than expected and the Federal reserve had begun to raise interest rates.

From 2006 through 2010, the economy was in transition but it took until 2007 for most to realize it. The last few years have seen the decline in real estate values from 10 to as much as 50 percent with the average since the peak in 2006 of a decline of 30 percent across the nation. People lost 40-50 percent of their value in the stock market just in the last couple of months of 2008. Millions of homeowners have been faced with foreclosure and the unemployment rate went over 10 percent. We have endured the longest and deepest recession since the Great Depression of 1929 and the government had to step in and become the banker as banks and Wall Street firms failed and lending tightened up. By 2008, our recession became a worldwide recession and nations around the world are now in the slow process of rebuilding their economies, opening up their lending environment again and getting back to positive growth.

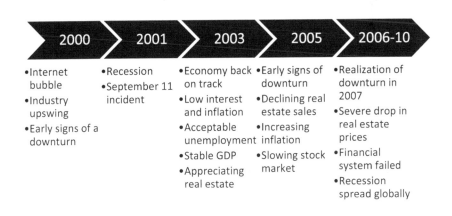

So what happened? Blindsided by the idea that there was a "new economy", that the old rules no longer applied and having access to too much easy money, many did not accept what the data was clearly showing—that the economy was spiralling downward. And in fact, everyone was using other people's money to fund their purchases and then leveraging even further on hyped up appreciated values, so once the bubbles burst and the money dried up it all came crashing down. So the greed of the last few years finally caught up with a world out of control.

What have we learned? We learned that it is not just about leveraging, IPOs, venture capitalists, fancy and complex lending structures, or bubbling real estate and stock markets. A successful, enduring economy is still more about the expansion of individual opportunity (small businesses), the energy of constant innovation (getting better at what you do), the power of technology and communications (information anyplace, anywhere, anytime) and the power of the customer.

What we did instead, dazzled by seemingly limitless returns, is allow banks to fund hundreds of companies and thousands of home mortgages to capture dubious markets, to assist unqualified borrowers to buy homes, and to let people margin their way into the stock market driving company and real estate values and shares prices to unheard limits.

So, now starts the return to sanity and the rebuilding. People will be pushed onto the train, so expect more taxation, deeper government regulations, conservative lending, less appreciation in both the real estate and stock markets, and slower growth in the economy.

And recessions are not a thing of the past, our economy will still have boom and bust cycles but this one has hopefully taught us that there are no "new economies"– there are only old economies with new twists. This last recession happened very quickly, it was led by a sharp fall off in capital investment and a slump in consumer spending. So if nothing else, this last recession has shown us that economies are still fluid systems and thus they are the ultimate stress test for how solid is the economic foundation upon which they play out their havoc.

THE PRESENT AND FUTURE OF ECONOMY

Our economy today is so much more layered and complex than it has ever been.

First it is global—we buy goods from around the world and send them our dollars as payment. They then send those dollars back to us by buying our treasuries which puts money into our system so that we can buy their goods again. At the same time most countries around the world peg their currencies against our dollar enabling currencies are stable. Governments buy and sell their currencies and then buy and sell dollars all to keep the monetary systems around the world in sync.

Second, our economy is no longer just about products and services. It is impacted by hedge plays, derivative manipulations, terrorist activities, natural disasters, political influences, Federal, state and local rules and regulations, global competition so our idea of our "free market" economy is not quite as free as it used to be.

Third, America for the first time seems to be divided almost 50:50 between free marketers versus socialists and conservatives versus liberals and this impacts the economy in many ways. Free marketers and conservatives like freer markets, less government, fewer rules, lower taxes and more individual choices. Socialists and liberals tend to want more regulated markets, more government involvement, increased selective taxation and fewer individual choices. Then there is the growing number of independents who can be conservative on some issues but liberal on others. No matter where you fit on the spectrum, the fact that more and more people are reaching out to the extremes rather than staying in the middle impacts not only the social fibre of America but also our economy. Think the environment and drilling for oil, gun control versus the NRA, the tobacco companies versus the non smoking, and fatty foods versus non fatty foods—the push is on from both sides with the economy getting squeezed in the middle.

Fourth, the economy today changes in seconds not years. The internet has meant that people and information can connect anytime, anyplace, anywhere 24/7. When information is instantaneous so are the decisions that result.

Fifth, the financial markets, lending, mergers, stock options, insider trading, restricted stock programs, nation and international currencies plays, the stock markets, the bond markets are so much complex and instant today. They are no longer time sensitive but time critical.

For the major stimulus, year adjustments in fiscal policy, inventories, profitability of companies, lending and the Fed's strategy will create a conflicting pattern of economic growth and financial changes. Thus, the outlook will be for a moderate economic recovery with some inflation. However, the recovery pattern could be very volatile from quarter to quarter and growth will be not be in a straight line upward.

Recovery after this recession will be below that of typical recessions due to continuing high unemployment, weak consumer spending, subpar business investment, tightened lending, slow rebounding real estate markets both residential and commercial and continuing government intervention and additional regulation.

The outlook for the next several years is a growing federal deficit—$1.4 trillion for 2010, overall at 11 trillion which places an additional burden on economic recovery. Add to that some inflation and subpar growth of 2 percent GDP and looking forward this economy will rebound but not be driving on all cylinders. Housing will continue to bottom out but foreclosures and short sales will be in the system for the next two years making up about 40 percent of all sales. Mortgage lending will ease up slightly but conservative underwriting criteria will be the new order of the day. We will be hearing about the commercial market too for the next few years out. Vacancies in 2010 will reach 25 percent and rents will decrease 20 percent from their highs. Eventually, by 2011 large groups of investors will enter both the distressed residential and commercial markets buying properties for pennies on the dollar. The consumer will start to spend again but only moderately and saving will be the new rallying cry moving forward. The consumer will also be a different shopper, no longer willing to shop until they drop. Value and discounting will become the main drivers of buying decisions. And they will be targeted on "have to buy items" rather than "want to buy items".

None of this is surprising anymore, so where will the surprise come from. The biggest surprise will be the government—increases in taxes (to which group and how much), more government regulation (what kind and over what industries), bigger government, the final outcome of bills like health care and cap and trade (what will they cost, who will they affect both positively and negatively), when if ever will the government get out of the stimulus business, and what will they do about job creation, the deficit and the eroding value of the dollar. More than anything this "new, expanded" role of government is causing uncertainty. Then you add in the global economic recession, violence in many areas around the world and we are in a unique economic situation, one we and others have never really experienced before.

It seems that today and moving forward we can move at the speed of light but where are we going? We communicate instantly but is anyone really listening? We produce more goods and services but are they really better? All of this can best be understood if we go back to the boom and bust cycles of the economy. We are now in that transition period from the boom cycle of the 1990s and this transition will last until 2020 and then we will move into a new boom cycle. The transition will be choppy, and mystifying. And yet, our economy is always searching for the next big thing. It could come from the greening environment, from new sources of energy or from biotech but it will come and cause the next revolution and change our economy once again.

And if the world seems a little crazy that is probably because it is—its bigger (we are global) but smaller (we are more connected), its more complex and yet all the gadgets we are urged to buy say they will make life simpler for us, we are working harder and longer but seem to get less for it. It's almost as if the world is a labyrinth of mazes each in contradiction to each other

But remember what goes up has to come down and what goes around comes around. No economy, no market has ever succeeded in overcoming economic cycles or waves. We will never reach a perfect economy or world—there are just too many different ideas of what defines perfect.

So looking forward, keep your eye on inflation, big brother, taxation, a move towards more government, terrorism, erosion of our individual freedoms, the redistribution of wealth and less values. Perhaps one of our forefathers said it best—the future should belong to those who earn it not to those who just want to take it.

So what about 2011?

Gross Domestic Product (GDP) will be positive but mild at 2% for the year, a slower than expected improvement. Still GDP will be pressured by what many are calling a jobless recovery which means that we will have positive GDP numbers with no job growth and thus not enough power in the economy to increase the GDP numbers over time.

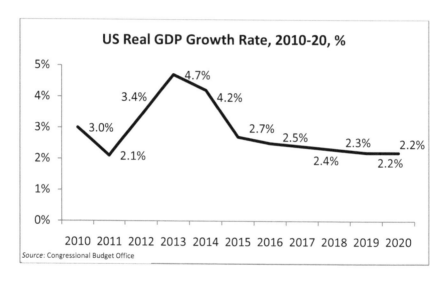

Inflation will be tame for most of the year but will begin to increase by year-end. The Federal Reserve will start to increase interest rates by year-end in an attempt to control increasing inflation.

The stock market will be positive in 2011 and the Dow should be at or above 10,000. Large cap stocks should do well as value will be the name of the game. The techs will also rebound and discount retailers like Target, Costco and Wal-Mart will do well but high-end boutiques and department stores will continue to have a difficult year. Airlines will still be struggling and the oil and gas industries' profits will lag 2010 mostly as a result of price turbulence and the international political picture. The hotel and restaurant industry will slowly show signs of recovery but not to the levels they enjoyed in past years— the increase will mostly come from price discounts and special offers. The brokerage industry will have some winners and some losers. Mergers and acquisitions will be better than in 2010 but still down from prior years, IPOs are still scarce, most of the companies will stop laying off employees, some will even start hiring. The banks will also have winners and losers—those that have repaid the tarp money can do more creative financing, those that have not will be hampered by higher debt on their balance sheet and government intervention.

Oil will range from the high 80's to the mid 90's.

The commodities bubble will continue to increase—think gold, copper, silver, etc...

The dollar will stay in the low range until the Federal Reserve starts to pull back liquidity from the market and starts to raise interest rates. The dollar will still be the currency of choice but it will be more turbulent in 2011 moving up and down more often. In fact, the dollar has been volatile since 1971 when we went off the gold standard. We now have a "fiat: currency which means that the dollar is not based on gold bullion but is based solely against "the full faith and credit of the US government". Through the late 1980s and early 1990s the dollar traded within a fairly narrow range but by the mid 1990s the US economy had surged ahead of the rest of the world and the dollar soared. Then when the US entered this last recession the dollar depreciated about 35% from its peak. Some worry that because of this some foreign investors will be less willing to place their money here but so far that has not proven to be the case. In fact, some economists see this decline, as long as it is moderate over time, as a healthy correction from unsustainably high levels. More than the value of the dollar our high deficit is the real problem.

Unemployment will stay at 8.5% - 9.5% percent throughout 2011 and probably will not rebound fully until 2013 or 2014. The reason goes beyond the unemployment numbers—it also has to do with average hours worked per week that are now at 34 hours per week and not 40 hours per week. That means that when companies begin to gear up again they will bring existing employees up to 40 hours per week rather than hire new employees. In addition, when people re rehired what kinds of jobs can they get—will the income levels of the new jobs replace their former income and will the jobs be in the same industries?

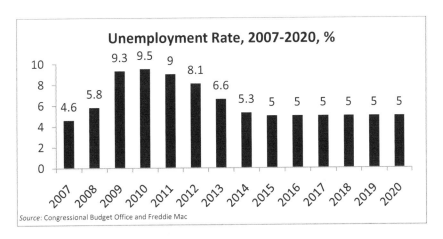

The economy will continue to rebound but it will be a mild rebound. Many firms are still debt heavy; the consumer is saving rather than spending. And our business models are so much more complex coming into 2011. Companies don't just make a product or provide a service anymore. They also provide financing to their buyers, they operate trading markets, they use options to hedge rapid price changes and they do business around the world.

The global economy will also rebound this year but except for China, India and Brazil their recoveries will also be mild.

Health care costs will continue to rise with premiums up around 8-9 percent. Many companies in anticipation of universal health care will drop retiree programs, shift more costs to employees and look for doctors, hospitals and health care insurance companies to readjust costs as much as they can before the new universal health care program state in 2013.

State budgets will continue to be squeezed this year too. States will continue to furlough employees, limit programs, tap into rainy day funds, and introduce ideas like taxing marijuana use, opening more casinos and of course raising taxes.

In all, a better year than 2010 but not great. There will be ups and downs, some green shoots but some hiccups. We will still feel like we are in recession and we will be—technically out but still deep into many of the issues like risk, over leverage, high debt levels, etc. —things that take years not just one year to correct.

IS HOMEOWNERSHIP STILL THE AMERICAN DREAM?

To understand why owning a home has been known as the American dream, we have to look back in time and analyze the asset—real estate, how it works and study why owning a home has built wealth for people over the last 50 plus years.

First and foremost, real estate is an asset where the value is found in the land (90%). That's why people always talk about location, location, and location. Whatever you build on top of the land can add or subtract from its value but unless the land has value going in, its appreciation will be more not less over time.

Second, real estate is a local phenomenon—that means that the local environment (supply and demand, local laws and regulations, the local economy) determine the state of the real estate market (strong versus correcting).

Third, real estate is in a constantly fluctuating state. About once every decade, the market finds itself in a sellers' market (easy access to money, low interest rates, more demand than supply) and properties often sell over list price with multiple offers. These markets usually last about 12-18 months and then the market corrects itself and moves to the buyer side of the market (a more balanced amount of supply and demand, higher interest rates and fair market value offers). The transition from a seller's market to a buyer's market usually takes the form of what many perceive as a "correcting market" where sales decrease, valuations go down about 5-10 percent and then the market finds a new price point floor foundation and prices stabilize before beginning to appreciate again. This whole process takes between 24-36 months.

Fourth, in a traditional real estate market, buyers find a home, put down 10-20 percent down payment and then finance the balance with the expectation that it will take 5-7 years for the property to appreciate enough in value for them to get a positive return on their investment. This process has worked very well for the last 50 years until 2000 when the guidelines of how to buy and finance a home changed.

In the year 2000, we were in a recession and the government trying to keep the economy from going into deep slump, moved aggressively to push home ownership as the way out of the recession. And from 2000-2005 it worked—home ownership went from 56% to almost 70% and home values across the US appreciated in some places as much as 100%. It was also easier to buy than rent as low interest rates and soft underwriting meant that anyone could get a loan. Everyone fell in love with real estate and people began using their homes as ATM machines cashing out often and spinning their properties two or three times a year. People also got into the real estate investment business, running to trendy areas in Florida, Nevada and Colorado buying as much as they could leverage because these areas provided them with inexpensive and "hot" properties. Two million more buyers sought out real estate as "the pot of gold at the end of the rainbow". In order to qualify for the loans on these properties, lenders had to lower their underwriting standards and zero down adjustable rates and negative amortization loans became the order of the day. Prices appreciated, which made people *feel* wealthier and so people started taking on more debt, buying expensive things like cars, and taking exotic vacations.

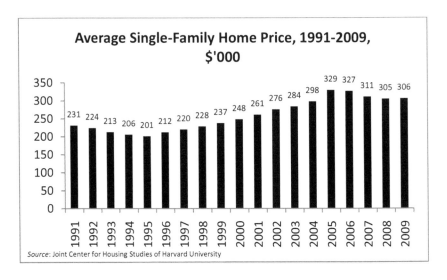

Everyone thought it was a new real estate world—it wasn't and the signs were out there as early as 2005 when sales started to decrease. Inventories grew and prices started to decline but since it was gradual at first, no one took much notice. It was not until there was an increase in foreclosures and large numbers of loans started to sour that people began to take notice. The first real wakeup call came from a company, New Century, which was a publicly traded mortgage company on the New York Stock Exchange. They did $50 billion in subprime loans the last year they were in business and of those only 1 out of every 4 borrowers ever made their first mortgage payment. The company was forced into bankruptcy and delisted from the New York Stock Exchange. Next came word that banks like Washington Mutual, and Wachovia were experiencing severe credit problems and then Wall Street with the failure of Bear Sterns joined in. Credit tightened and the housing market went from a normal slow decline into a freefall. In some areas properties began to decline as much as 5-10% a month and since the peak in 2006 the average decline has been 30% across the USA.

So can we say so much for the American dream—was it really the dream that blew up or how people lived the dream?

The New Real Estate Dream

More than anything it was not real estate but the fact that we changed the process (how you buy real estate) that changed the model—instead of 10-20% down we allowed people to get in with 0% down, the underwriting was relaxed and people took advantage.

We have been trying to get back to a stable, traditional market since 2005, and we are still trying to find a bottom. This past year has seen everything from stable markets, robust markets, declining markets, really depressed markets sometimes within a few miles of each other. In some areas the market is hot with multiple offers, in other markets it is dead in the water. Some markets get multiple offers, others get no offers. But still we can say, yes the market generally is better. All the indexes show us that month-to-month comparisons sales are growing and prices in many areas are stabilizing. And yet, beyond the stats we know that there are millions of more foreclosures coming, the tax credits for buyers ended in 2010 and loans are still difficult to get. So it is a mixed bag when the market will bottom—in some areas as soon as next year but in depressed areas not until 2015. In addition, when markets start to appreciate again the appreciation will be mild for several years out—think 2-3% not the usual 6-8% we have experienced in the San Francisco Bay Area.

So predictions for the 2011 real estate market are more positive than negative here, however, the degree of improvement will be based on a variety of influences. The tendency is to want to generalize market conditions but that will not work this year, the year of the "new" American dream.

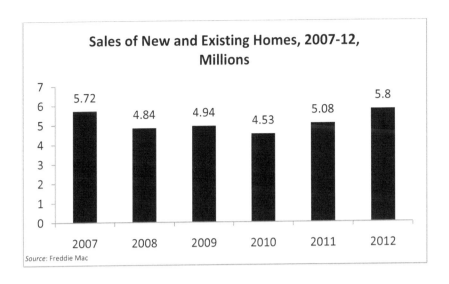

Sales of New and Existing Homes, 2007-12, Millions

Source: Freddie Mac

First, improvement will depend on the type of real estate it is—single family, condominium, town house, multi-units, or commercial.

Second, the location of the real estate and whether the property is in the entry-level market or the higher end will determine improvement or not

Third, the amount of the loan and getting the loan will be important

Fourth, the amount of inventory—not just the number but what kind of inventory from regular sales, to foreclosures or short sales—each makes a difference to valuation in their markets.

Fifth, the appraisal and whether or not the property will appraise for what the buyer is willing to pay is critical—think of it as value (what the buyer will pay versus valuation what the appraisal will show) and often there is a disconnect between the two in this new real estate market.

Sixth, in specific markets the number of rentals versus owner occupied, the financial state of condominiums, etc. will all influence the markets for years.

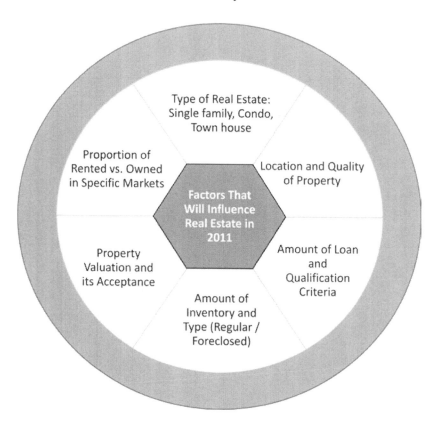

So the dream that was so strong and clear over the last 50 years has faded but is not gone. It is still there but it is the new American dream.

The New Dream

The new dream is a hybrid—part of the old traditional model—more conservative again, with structured loan products that require good FICO scores and a reasonable down payment and the understanding that one needs to stay in a property at least 5 years. At the same time, the new model is vastly different too. The seller today is not the neighbor down the street, with 45% of all sales in the US linked to foreclosures and short sales (in the SF Bay Area it is 25%). In fact, the major seller is now the bank. Banks are a business seller, they time inventory, they control appraisals and they "create" market environments rather than consumers who have to respond to market environments. Banks will be in this new real estate market for at least the next 3-4 years and projections say another 2 million foreclosures will pass through the ranks. The banks also strongly control the buyers side of all markets—foreclosures, the mid tier market and the high end—because of their oversight of the appraisal process. Since May, 2008 most appraisers work for bank owned asset management companies and thus their guidelines are set by the banks not market conditions. And if a property doesn't appraise at the same price that a buyer is willing to offer the deal falls through.

At the same time, the profile of the buyer has changed from the old American dream market. Yes, the first time buyer still makes up the majority of the market at >45% but in the new American dream market we have lost at least 20% of the organic or move up buyer. Now too investors with cash make up at least 20% of the market. These investors have different goals for the new American dream—they want to purchase inexpensive properties that they can rent with positive cash flow on day one or they want appreciation in less than the normal 5-7 year period.

Also, the lending market today is different from the old American dream market. In the old days loans were written down at your local bank branch were they knew you personally. Today, loans are done through software run by FHA, Fannie Mae or Freddie Mac. They have strict underwriting guidelines that review the application online and either you qualify or you don't. Gone are the personal relationships and today all is based against evaluation models.

There are also new competitors in the new American dream market:

- The banks

- The developers
- The cash client
- The international buyer and seller
- The investor funds or groups

In the old American dream market it was mostly a client to a client market but today in the new American dream market it can be client-to-client, business to client, investor to investor, client to investor etc....This makes the process much more complex and competitive.

The lifestyle of Americans and who they are has also changed. And this has impacted the new market. In the past there was a push from the cities into the suburbs. Today people want to live all over—in the suburbs, in the cities, in assisted living in retirement communities, in rural areas etc. Children live at home longer today too, some parents are buying homes for their children and some parents live with their children in family home environments. The face of American is also changing—minorities now make up much of the American landscape with Hispanics and Asians the fasting growing demographics.

Also in the old American dream market the inventory was simple—mostly single family homes with a few apartments. Today we have single family homes, condominiums, town homes, and mobile homes. Sprawl is out and density building and greening is in. Today permits are harder to get, zoning is more restrictive and everything takes more time and money. Many buyers are also interested in the small commercial markets those 1-4 units, small apartment complexes or strip malls as well as investing in foreign areas. Thus markets are tiered, offering more choices but greater complexity in determining where the best areas are, which type of investments are the best, which markets are hot and which will appreciate sooner and by how much.

The buyer pool has also expanded. In the old American dream market most buyers were families. Today single women and single men are among the fastest growing segment of the market.

Lastly, the way real state will appreciate in the new American dream market will be different than under the old model. It will be milder and take longer.

So is the dream Dead?

No the dream is not dead it is just different. Real estate is still a very desirable asset

- You can get in reasonably easy
- The government subsidizes your mortgage on a principal residence

- In the right location it will appreciate over time
- The government gives you many tax benefits—especially the 121 which is allowed on a principal residence if you have owned it 2 out of the last five years tax free appreciation of up to $250,000 if you are single and $500,000 if you are married.

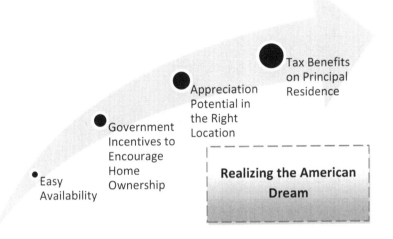

The real estate market today is more tiered, more complex, with varying conditions and values and many more influences impacting it. So the key is to understand the markets, to get educated, do your research, work with professionals and remember that the most important things to the American dream are:

- To buy in the right location (think land)
- To get a "safe" loan (invest in the property and get one that buffers you for the downtimes)

- To expect to keep the property for at least 5-7 years so that you can ride out any changes in the markets
- To understand the difference between value (what a buyer is willing to pay) versus valuation (what an appraiser determines a property is worth)
- To know why you are purchasing a property. Is it to live in, as an investment to rent or as an investment (to turn over quickly)? All this means you have different goals which means different pricing strategies, different markets, different opportunities.
- To get into markets where there is opportunity—upside potential not just cheap markets
- And to be certain that you have made a "smart" decision not just an emotional decision

You do all of this and you have the American dream.

PAST, PRESENT AND FUTURE OF REAL ESTATE

Overview

The US Real Estate Market mirrors the status of the nation's economy, both having picked up in the last one year. Although data indicates further improvement in the housing market in 2011, there are analysts who attribute the growth to temporary government interventions such as the home buyer tax credit.

New job additions and rock bottom home prices - two essential factors for sustained economic recovery have contributed to the uptick in real estate in 2010. However, the role of incentives such as the home buyer tax credit cannot be undermined. It fuelled the initial rebound in 2009 and as the incentive was later recalled, it took the home sales with it. The market remained sluggish in the first quarter of 2010 and bounced again when the tax credit incentive was re-introduced.

The year 2010 observed volatility both in residential real estate prices and sales led by policy changes. Third quarter saw a rise in sales compared to the previous quarters but the beginning of the fourth quarter faced trend reversal. The sales in the first ten months of 2010 were down 2.9% compared with the same period in the previous year.

Despite the unplugging of the government incentive, factors such as high housing affordability, low mortgage rates, improving employment data and GDP growth are likely to propel the housing market out of the woods in the coming years.

Historical Real Estate Prices

The housing market saw a sharp decline in home prices since 2008 and the trend is expected to continue to remain subdued until the next few years. The situation presents an interesting dichotomy:

- On one hand the low home prices, coupled with other factors, have made it quite tempting for a section of citizens to shop for their dream abode.
- On the other hand about one in seven homeowners now owe more on their mortgages than their homes are worth, shaking commitment to their homes.

The latter has caused the seriously delinquent loans to go on a record high and foreclosures exceeded 2 million by 2009 end. As a result, the banks have become weary of lending making it relatively difficult for the first category of citizens to realize their dream.

According to the S&P/Case-Shiller Home Price Index data for the year 2010, end of third quarter saw a reversal in trend when the real estate prices in 20 US cities grew at the slowest pace compared with the previous two quarters, leading some analysts to believe that the housing market is on the brink of another slowdown. The demand-supply gap widened as the supply continued to grow supported by foreclosures while the demand contracted as a result of the expiration of tax credit incentive. Among the 20 cities that form the index, Chicago, in 2010, saw the steepest decline of 5.6% on a year-over-year basis while San Francisco underwent the biggest rise at 5.5% during the same period.

Affordability Index

About The Index

Housing Affordability Index (HAI) indicates whether or not a standard family could qualify for a mortgage loan on a standard home. A standard home is defined as the national median priced, existing single-family home while a standard family is defined as one earning the median family income as declared by the US Bureau of Census.

An affordability index of 100 suggests that a family with the median income has exactly enough income to qualify for a mortgage on a median-priced home. An index over 100 means that a family earning the median income has more than enough income to qualify for a mortgage loan on a median-priced home, assuming a 20 percent down payment. As an example, an affordability index of 120 means a family earning the median family income has 120% of the income necessary to qualify for a mortgage covering 80 percent of a median-priced existing single-family home. Hence, a rise in the HAI shows that a family is more able to afford the median priced home.

Rising Housing Affordability

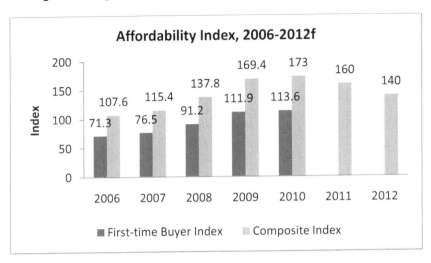

Affordability Index, 2006-2012f

In 2010, housing affordability remained high facilitated by low mortgage rates and dwindling home prices. The fundamentals of a pickup in housing demand remain in place in the forms of job creation numbers and high affordability. Even though investors appear tempted to leverage the situation, they are being hindered by strict guidelines for non-owner occupancy mortgage.

The home buyer tax credit, originally meant for the first-time home buyers, boosted their affordability as evident in data that shows 50 percent of all home buyers between July 2009 and June 2010 were first time buyers against an average of 40-41% over the last decade.

The economic downturn shook the buyer landscape and has potentially opened up the housing market for those who originally could not afford a home. Although the median household income of home buyers declined nationally over the last two years, but at the same time, mortgage interest rates dropped to historically low levels along with the declining home prices. As a result, the decline in the median household income of home buyers reflects how improved housing affordability – coupled with government incentives supporting home-buying – opened the market to a new segment of the American demographic landscape.

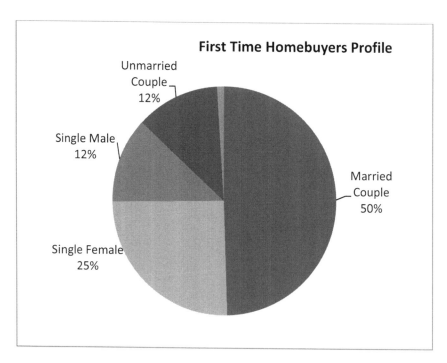

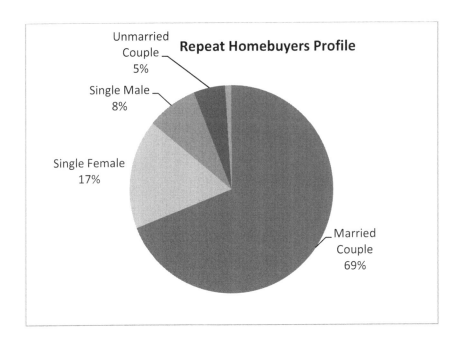

Repeat Homebuyers Profile

Unmarried Couple 5%

Single Male 8%

Single Female 17%

Married Couple 69%

As some surveys have showed, affordability as a motivating factor has increased among both the first time buyers and the repeat buyers largely for buyers who are under 44 years of age.

Homeownership Rate

Homeownership rate, simply defined as the ratio of owner occupied homes by the total number of occupied homes, declined in 2007 and 2008 and remained steady in 2009. The decline in 2007 and 2008 was attributed to the foreclosures while in 2009 the foreclosures were somewhat matched by the first-time home buyers.

In 2009, homeownership rates dropped in all 4 regions of the country and in over 60 percent of the states. The most significant drop occurred in the Midwest, where the rate stood 2.8 percentage points below its peak in 2004. The Northeast recorded the least decline.

Although the drop in homeownership has adversely impacted households of all incomes but the worst affected are the low-income families. This group had previously achieved a better growth in ownership rates compared to the higher-income households. During 1995-2009, the homeownership rates among the bottom income quartile grew 6 percentage points while rates for the higher-income households rose 4 percentage points. However, during 2005-2009, homeownership rates for the low-income households fell twice as much as those for the higher-income households on a percentage point basis.

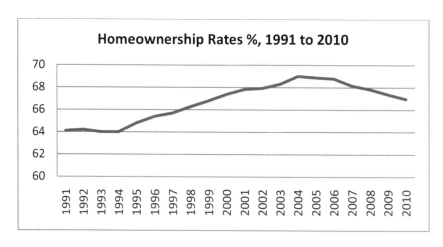

Among the states, West Virginia leads the pack with the highest homeownership rate of 78.7% in 2009. The state has maintained its status over the last decade and has continued its leading position in the first three quarters of 2010. Closely followed by West Virginia are Delaware, New Hampshire, Idaho and Mississippi in the top five. The states occupying the bottom 5 positions include District of Columbia, New York, California, Hawaii and Nevada. California had a homeownership rate of 57% in 2009 which further dropped in 2010 and stood at 56.2 percent in the third quarter. Among the 51 states and districts, California stood 49th in terms of homeownership rate in 2009 and improved one rank to 48 in the third quarter in 2010 as Hawaii dropped one position.

The consistent low ranking in homeownership rate of California is explained by the remarkably high cost of real estate in the state. Homeownership rates are lower in principal cities, 52.6 percent compared with rates over 70 percent in suburbs and non-metro areas.

Homeownership rate varies with the race; Whites had the highest rate at 74.8% in 2009, followed by Asian Americans (59.3%), Native Americans (56.2%), Hispanics (48.4%) and African Americans (46.2%) in the same year.

Foreclosure Trends and Forecast

Housing Predictor, a real estate research firm, reduced its forecast for the number of foreclosures by 3.5 million through to 2015. Post the revision of the forecast, the number of foreclosures by 2015 is expected to be 16.5 million. The actual number of foreclosures, however, is expected to remain high as lenders look to speed up recovery and in the process will overlook households that might find themselves in a position to repay their mortgages in the future.

Towards the end of 2010, the government enforced a moratorium on foreclosures as a step to halt shoddy recovery practices by the lenders. Although it gave some breathing space to the homeowners, it is suspected that the guideline will only delay the inevitable. On the contrary, the moratorium threatened further delay in recovery as homes slated for repossession took longer to come to market.

According to the National Association of Realtors, the U.S. housing sector has undergone about 4-5 million foreclosures since the start of the recession. That number would continue to grow once major lenders resume their temporarily suspended foreclosure operations.

According to RealtyTrac, in the fourth quarter of 2010 foreclosure activity in the US was the highest in California at 66,475. The top four states in foreclosures after California were Florida, Michigan, Illinois and Arizona. Although foreclosure sales declined from the second to the third quarter in 2010, they still accounted for about 25 percent of overall homes sales in the third quarter.

During 2009 and 2010 the government took a series of steps to help curb foreclosures or at least delay the process of foreclosures:

- Federal and state loss mitigation programs and moratoriums
- Policy changes to increase the number of refinances through government subsidized loans from Fannie Mae and Freddie Mac to facilitate cut in the number of homeowners at risk
- Mortgage modifications that touched 2.4 million
- Federal programs giving temporary aid to unemployed mortgage holders

TransUnion, a leading credit ratings agency, predicts that US mortgage delinquency rates will witness a double digit decline in 2011. This will be driven by an improving economy and a stabilizing real estate market, as more homeowners get up to date on their mortgage payments.

Mortgage delinquency rates, which rose by 50 percent each year from 2006 to 2009, are expected to fall in all 50 states by over 10% in 2011. This appears to be an extremely positive outlook given the mayhem in the mortgage market with foreclosures and rising inventory clouding the sector in 2010.

The TransUnion report estimates that the mortgage delinquency rate will drop to 4.98% in 2011, from 6.21% in 2010.

According to TransUnion, mortgage delinquency rate peaked at 6.89% during the fourth quarter of 2009 but closed the year 2010 with moderate improvement at 6.2%. A decrease in mortgage delinquencies, typically a precursor to foreclosure, will boost the fledgling recovery in the US economy and the residential real-estate market.

Mortgage delinquency for loans that were at least one payment past due also improved to 9.13 percent from 9.85 percent in the second quarter of 2010. This rate was 4.95% when the housing boom at its peak in 2006.

Even the serious mortgage delinquencies declined in October 2010 from its highs in 2009, according to Fannie Mae. Despite the expected decline in mortgage delinquency, the absolute numbers still remain high as the unemployment rate continues to remain high at around 10%.

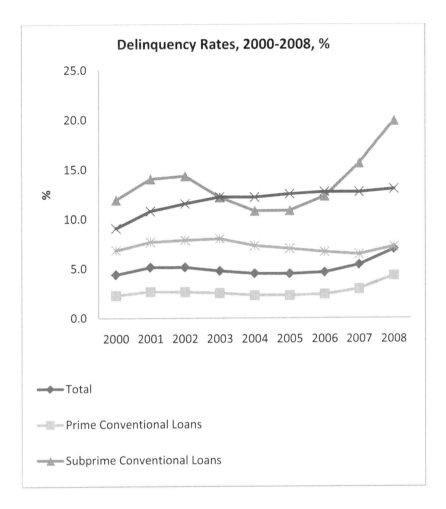

By the end of 2009, about one in seven owners owed more on their mortgage loan than their homes were worth as a result of which foreclosures exceeded two million. According to the National Association of Realtors, over a third of existing home sales last year — approximately 1.8 million units — were foreclosure led. Foreclosures have eased in the last few months partly because of new legislation passed by the Obama administration that has made it more difficult for lenders to move owners out of their homes. And many lenders temporarily slowed or halted their foreclosure activities, after legal challenges successfully raised questions about the propriety of the procedures they had been following.

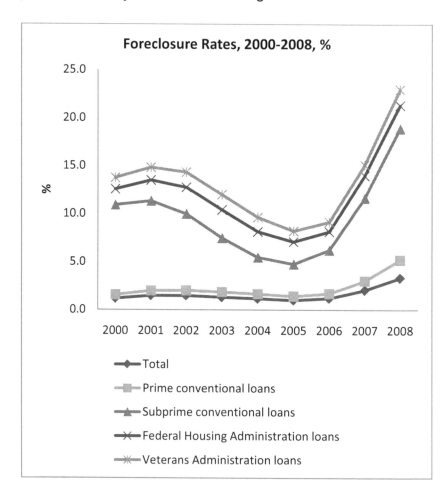

Ranking of cities with highest foreclosure rates in the US vary depending on the analyst's assessment. However, California, Florida, Nevada and Arizona consistently feature as the highest contributing states to foreclosure. According to RealtyTrac, these four states accounted for 19 of the 20 major cities with the highest foreclosure rate in the third quarter of 2010. The 10 major cities with highest foreclosure rates were:

- Las Vegas-Paradise, Nevada, with one in 25 households receiving notices
- Cape Coral-Fort Myers, Florida, one in 35 households
- Modesto, California, one in 36 households
- Stockton, California, one in 39 households
- Merced, California, one in 40 households
- Riverside-San Bernardino-Ontario, California, one in 41 households
- Miami-Fort Lauderdale-Pompano Beach, Florida, one in 41 households
- Phoenix-Mesa-Scottsdale, Arizona, one in 44 households
- Bakersfield, California, one in 44 households
- Vallejo-Fairfield, California, one in 45 households

Net Worth Tied to Housing

According to a research by Zillow, homes in 2010 lost more cumulative value than they did in 2009, denting hopes of revival in the housing market. The residential market lost $1.7 trillion in 2010 which is 63 percent more than $1 trillion lost in 2009.

In comparison to the peak values in June 2006, over $9 trillion in values disappeared from the housing market. According to a study by the Congressional Research Service, extent of this loss is equivalent to the cost of 12 wars in Iraq.

Although this steep fall in net worth for a homeowner is disappointing, the actual implications in the broader context vary depending upon the situation of each homeowner:

- A big dollar figure doesn't necessarily mean a big average drop in home values. The value in New York saw a decline by $103.7 billion but the city has a huge number of homes - approximately 4 million residential units. As a result, the median home values fell by a modest 3.8 percent year-on-year.

- Some cities like Boston and San Diego actually witnessed a rise in total market value, driven primarily by the homebuyer tax credits.
- The loss could just be notional if the homeowner plans to stay in the house for years to come, hence apart from causing a mental dissatisfaction, a drop in price is not actually a loss.
- The homeowner could have bought a property in a different era altogether and may still be able to sell and move out by making a marginal profit.
- However, in a scenario when a homeowner wants to sell or refinance, the current value of their property becomes more important. Any of those activities may still be possible, as long as the homeowner has positive equity, but in the case of negative equity, he will find himself trapped.

Government interventions, like the homebuyers credit, did help buoy the market in the first half of 2010, but once those came to an end, the market again began to slide. Because of the high rates of foreclosure and negative equity, the first half of 2011 is not expected to bring much relief. However, the hope is that the market will bottom-out sometime in 2011, and that average rates of appreciation will return sometime in the next three to five years.

PAST, PRESENT AND FUTURE OF LENDING

After years of record-setting originations, proliferation of new products, and tolerance of lax underwriting, mortgage lending did an about-face in 2007 and 2008. According to Freddie Mac estimates, originations fell by 33 percent in real terms in 2008 alone and by 62 percent from the 2003 level (See the origination volume chart later in this chapter). Non-prime lending (including subprime and near-prime loans) went from a flood to a trickle before the spigot was effectively shut off.

Originations of non-prime loans with so-called affordability features—such as interest-only or payment-option loans—also plunged, falling from almost 20 percent of originations in 2005 to less than 2 percent in 2008 to near zero in 2010.

The drop-off was particularly sharp in states and metropolitan areas where these loans were especially popular. For example, the share of loans with affordability features originated in San Francisco, San Jose, and San Diego exceeded 50 percent during the peak of the housing boom. Similarly, "piggyback" loans went from more than a third of all home purchase loans in 2006 to almost nothing by the end of 2010.

Fannie Mae and Freddie Mac, operating under federal conservatorship, now dominate the market along with government-owned FHA and Ginnie Mae. After elimination of Sub-prime mortgages and reluctance of Banks and investors to lend with their own money, these Government entities now control more than 95% of US Mortgage originations.

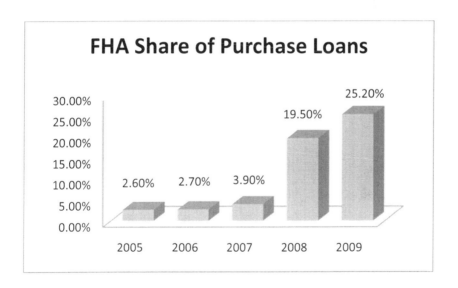

Lower interest rates and relaxed loan-to-value standards at Fannie Mae and Freddie Mac sparked a wave of refinancing in 2009 and 2010, indicating that private primary market activity can ramp up quickly. But before the market for loans lacking implicit or explicit federal guarantees can revive, investors must be willing to purchase these loans—or the securities they back—without such large risk premia. By the time these private label markets do come back, it is likely that the federal government will have taken actions to prevent another collapse.

Because of tighter lending guidelines, only a limited pool of households can take advantage of today's soft home prices. Current homeowners do not benefit from lower prices if their own homes are also worth less, and first-time buyers must overcome higher hurdles to qualify for mortgages. Indeed, the renewal of strict underwriting standards has turned back the clock on credit access for first-time homebuyers by about 15 years, restoring the income and wealth constraints that were so much a focus of national housing policy in the 1990s.

Origination Volume: These are the worst of days for lending industry. After witnessing mind-boggling growth in the early part of the century (see chart on the next page), 2010 origination volume for residential mortgages was $1.5

trillion. If that's not bad enough, Mortgage Bankers Association (MBA) forecasts 2011 mortgage origination volume (for Residential Mortgages) to be under $1 trillion, lowest since 1996. Per MBA, 2012 would be no better and will again see volume under $1 trillion. The biggest hit will be to the Refinance business which was at 65% and 69% of the total origination in 2009 and 2010 respectively. That's expected to go down to 36% in 2011 and 24% in 2012. We think with the rise in interest rate, even 36% look stretched. The Refinance share could very well go down to 25% or less in 2011.

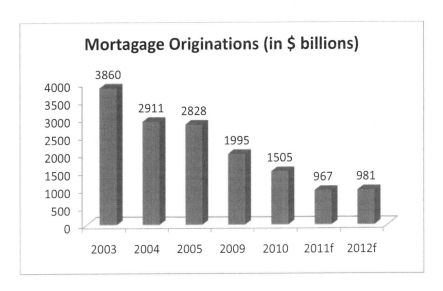

Interest Rates: There is a lot of misconception about what drives the mortgage rates, including the most common – it's the Fed rate that decides the mortgage rates. If you are not sure, watch the video here on what really impacts mortgage rates - http://lendingexpertblog.com/a-video-on-how-mortgage-interest-rates-move/.

We all know mortgage rates are at historically lowest levels. How low? See the chart to get an indication (source – Freddie Mac).

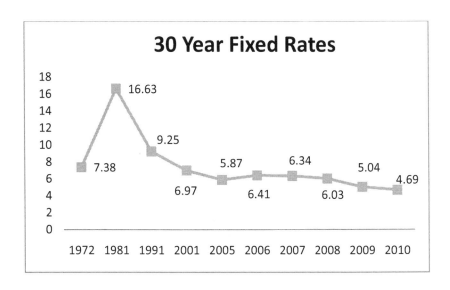

The big question is – for how long the interest rates will remain low? Interest rates like any other number needs to be looked at in relation to the history. And as the chart above suggests, even a rate in the 6s will be considered low from historical perspective. Forecasting mortgage rates could be very tricky. Having said that, we think the mortgage rates in 2011 will start climbing and will end the year between 5.25% - 5.5% and in 2012 it will be between 5.5%-6%. Whether this prediction turns out to be accurate or not, one thing seems certain the best rates that we saw for most part of 2010 are behind us.

On the face of it, for Real Estate industry saddled with excess inventory, high unemployment rate and tight lending guidelines, it might come across as another major hurdle. But don't be surprised if a lot of buyers who have been sitting on fence, having taken the low interest rate for granted may decide to purchase home after evaluating the risk of higher interest rates. Consider this scenario; a buyer who buys a $425,000 house at 5% interest rate (with 20% down) will pay a lower mortgage payment than someone who buys a $382,500 house at 6% interest rate. As you can see, the risk of rising interest rates is higher than waiting for real estate prices to fall further.

Sales Price	$425,000	$403,750	$382,500
Loan Amount	$410,125	$389,618	$369,112
Interest Rate	5.00%	5.50%	6.00%
P&I Payment	$2,240	$2251	$2,252

Major changes to Underwriting Guidelines: The biggest change in underwriting guidelines over last couple of years is not so much about higher down payments requirements, but some of the changes with the following:

Elimination of low/no income documentation requirements - What that means is most of the self-employed and people who work on commissions do not qualify for loans anymore, since now the net income (Gross income minus all expenses) documented on tax returns are used for qualifying. Worse still, high downpayment and excellent credit score alone are not compensating factors any more. Buyers still need to qualify for housing and debt ratios based on documented income even if they are putting in a large downpayment (in excess of 25%).

Condo Financing – Since April 2009 when Fannie Mae and Freddie Mac changed their condo guidelines, it's been a tough ride for securing financing for a Condominium. FHA followed suit sometime later and eliminated "spot approvals" which had earlier allowed loan approvals for any single unit even if the project was not approved. Some Condo underwriting guidelines which are now followed by

GSEs (Government sponsored enterprises i.e. Fannie Mae and Freddie Mac) and HUD are as follows:

Higher Interest Rate/Cost: There is now a .75% pricing adjustment by Fannie and Freddie for all loans >75% LTV secured by a condominium. So your buyers will either have to pay this in form of paying extra points or taking a higher interest rate to offset the cost.

Delinquent HOA Dues/Pending Litigation: No financing is allowed where more than 15% occupants of the attached condominium units are 30 days or more delinquent on their HOA dues. Also note that if there are any pending litigations against the HOA, it's not eligible for financing any more.

"Walls-in" coverage policy required: Earlier, if the Home Owner's Association (HOA) dues covered the Hazard insurance homebuyers didn't have to worry about buying additional insurance. Not anymore! The new guidelines ask for "Walls-in" coverage (also known as HO-6 policy). As the name suggests, this covers wall-to-wall insurance inside your house. The HO-6 insurance policy must provide coverage in an amount that is no less than 20 percent of the condominium unit's appraised value.

Owner-Occupancy Ratio Requirements: Both the GSEs and HUD have owner-occupancy requirements for condo financing, meaning a certain percentage of the units have to be owner-occupied. A project that has more units rented than owner-occupied may not qualify for financing.

Jumbo Financing – Getting financing for high-end homes continue to be challenging. Take the example of San Francisco Bay Area homes. In November 2010, 9.8 percent of the Bay Area's home purchase loans were ARMs, compared to the Bay Area's average monthly ARM rate over the last decade of 53 percent. Jumbo loans, mortgages above the old conforming limit of $417,000, accounted for 32.3 percent of November 2010 purchase lending. However, before the August 2007 credit crunch, jumbos accounted for nearly 60 percent of the Bay Area purchase loan market. For loan amounts above $729,750 (Conforming Jumbo loan limits), there are very few funding sources available and that too at higher downpayments (25% and higher) and a much higher interest rates (usually 1% or higher than the conforming rates). With the high-end real estate prices far from stabilized, banks and private investors are still wary of lending their money for jumbo loans. It could take a while (2-5 years) before we see normal lending return to Jumbo market.

Loan Level Price Adjustments (LLPAs) – LLPAs are add-ons to the rate and/or cost for the borrowers. LLPAs are assessed based upon certain loan features, including loan purpose, occupancy, number of units, product type, etc. In last couple of years while Fannie Mae and Freddie Mac have tightened their underwriting guidelines, they have also made it more expensive for some lesser qualified borrowers to get a loan. In the table below, you can see the impact a lower credit score can have on a borrower e.g. For a $400,000 loan amount, for a 80% loan a borrower with 659 credit score will pay $11,000 or 2.75% additional in closing cost compared to someone who has a 740 score.

Credit Score/LTV	70.01%-75%	75.01%-80%	80.01%-85%	85.01%-90%
>739	0.00%	0.25%	0.25%	0.25%
720-739	0.25%	0.50%	0.50%	0.50%
700-719	0.75%	1.00%	1.00%	1.00%
680-699	1.25%	1.75%	1.50%	1.25%
660-679	2.00%	2.50%	2.75%	2.25%
640-659	2.50%	3.00%	3.25%	2.75%

As mentioned above, there are other price add-ons based on property type, occupancy, product type etc. To get a complete list go to

https://www.efanniemae.com/sf/refmaterials/llpa/.

LITTLE KNOWN, NO TO LOW DOWNPAYMENT LOANS

With all these tightening of lending guidelines it's more important than ever that Real Estate agents and Loan Officers should be aware of specialty programs that can help potential buyers qualify when conventional loan programs don't work out.

Below are some of the loan programs that you should absolutely be aware of:

FHA Loans:

NAR reported that First Time Home Buyers now represent 50% of all home purchases (see chart) and it's estimated that 50% First Time Home Buyers now use FHA loans for home financing.

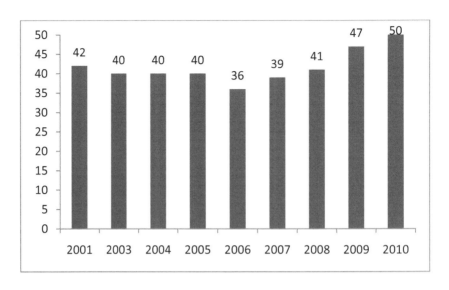

So what makes FHA loans so popular?

- Downpayment as low as 3.5%
- No Loan Level Price Adjustments (discussed earlier in this chapter)
- Income and assets of Non Occupying Co-borrowers can be used to qualify for the loan
- Loan Amount up to $729,750 (Varies by county)
- Entire downpayment can be gifted by a family member or even a close friend
- No Reserve requirements after closing
- Minimum credit score of 620 allowed

Even though FHA Loans have become unavoidable, some misconceptions still remain. Here are some myths:

1. *It takes longer to close an FHA Loan-* Towards the 2nd half of 2008 when FHA loans started exploding; most of the lenders were caught off guard. They did not have enough trained underwriters to take decisions on the loans that were being sent their way. That resulted in longer turn times for FHA loans. Within months, lenders realized that this was soon becoming the fastest mortgage product on the block. Since then they have staffed themselves adequately on the FHA underwriting side and hence it's not atypical anymore for FHA loans to close in 30 days or less.

2. *Interest Rates are higher* - While interests rates are situation specific and can potentially change multiple times just in a day, FHA loans are usually priced the same as conventional. In fact at the time of printing this book, FHA rates have been better than conventional for last 4-6 months.

3. *Closing Cost is higher* - FHA charges 1.00% up front Mortgage Insurance as closing cost. That could make you think that your buyer will have to bring that extra 1.00% to closing table. While that 1.00% is considered a closing cost, it's added to the loan amount, e.g. if your base loan amount was $400,000, your final loan amount actually becomes $404,000. As you can see FHA loans do not

increase the amount of closing cost that you need to bring at closing.

4. Income Limits to Qualify - To qualify for FHA loans there are absolutely no house hold income limits. Meaning you could be making $1 million a year (or more) and could still be eligible for an FHA loan.

5. Can't sell/refinance quickly- FHA loans just like most of the conventional loans have no Pre-payment Penalty. What that means is you can sell your house or refinance anytime you wish to after closing the transaction.

6. Appraisal Requirements are tougher - In December 2005, FHA made a number of changes to appraisal guidelines allowing for "As-Is" appraisals even if minor defects to the property conditions exist. FHA appraisals now only require repairs for conditions that rise above cosmetic defects, minor defects, or normal wear and tear. Mostly, the appraisal requirements now resemble that of Conventional mortgages.

7. FHA is only for First Time Home Buyers – FHA Loans are only for Owner Occupied properties, but the borrowers *do not* have to be first time home buyers. Trade up (or down) borrowers are eligible for FHA loans too, as long as they occupy the property as primary residence.

FHA 203K Rehab Loans:

Have your buyers found that "almost perfect" home in the right location that is selling at a reduced price because it needs a little rehab work?

Unfortunately, most mortgage loan programs require homes "in need of work" to be complete before the financing can be secured for the purchase transaction. Whether the property needs a little or a lot of work, most home buyers don't have the up-front cash to invest in a property prior to actually securing the financing. The FHA 203(k) Rehab Loan may be your answer to turning that "fixer-upper" into their dream home.

The FHA 203(k) Rehab Loan is a popular mortgage program created for buyers that want to finance the cost of home improvements into a new loan. The financing for this loan will include the purchase price, as well as the improvements required to do to be able to live in the home, and/or that the buyers want to do, such as upgrade the kitchen, bathroom, etc.

This is also a great loan program for agents trying to sell homes that need repair. Potential buyers will have an option to complete those repairs and upgrades without a large upfront financial commitment. Think of this as a one-time close construction loan. At closing, the seller receives their money and the rest is put into an escrow account for the buyer to use for rehabbing the property.

Two Types of FHA 203(k) Loans:

The *Streamlined K* is used when you want to make minor cosmetic changes to a house and the total rehab cost cannot exceed $35,000.
A *Standard FHA 203(k)* loan allows you to make substantial structural improvements, repairs; remodelling and updating to a house...even build a new one.

To find out more about 203k Rehab Loans go to - http://goo.gl/1hLWP

VA Loans:

The VA Loan Guaranty program is a benefit for our veterans. All veterans who served a required length of service and an acceptable character of service can receive it. The benefit of the veteran is the underlying principle. The VA may only guarantee a loan when it is possible to determine if the veteran

- Has sufficient VA entitlement available
- Is a satisfactory credit risk AND

- Has present and anticipated income sufficient for repayment of the mortgage and other living expenses

Some of the Home Buyer benefits of this loan:

- No Down Payment, 100% financing
- No monthly mortgage insurance premiums
- Leniency on credit and employment history
- No reserve requirements (1 unit only)
- Seller can pay off debt for borrower
- 100% gift funds allowed
- 2 years on Chapter 7 BK discharge
- 1 year on Chapter 13 BK pay out

To find out more about VA loans go to - http://goo.gl/dwijO

USDA Loans:

This loan is available only for homes located in rural areas. A rural area is any town with a population of 25,000 or less, that is not next to a metropolitan area. Some of the Home Buyer benefits of this loan:

- 100% LTV
- No Mortgage Insurance

- Don't have to be First Time Home Buyer
- No Loan Limit or Sale Price limit
- Unlimited Gifts allowed
- No Reserves required

In order to be eligible for many USDA loans, household income must meet certain guidelines. Also, the home to be purchased must be located in an eligible rural area as defined by USDA. Go to this link to check for income and property eligibility - http://goo.gl/zQUmo

HomePath Loans:

This special financing is available on foreclosed houses owned by Fannie Mae. The benefits include:

- Low down payment and flexible mortgage terms (fixed-rate, adjustable-rate, or interest-only)
- Buyers may qualify even if your credit is less than perfect
- Available to both owner occupiers and investors
- Down payment (at least 3 percent) can be funded by own savings; a gift; a grant; or a loan from a nonprofit organization, state or local government, or employer
- No mortgage insurance

- No appraisal fees

HomePath® Renovation Mortgage Financing is also available to finance both the home purchase and some renovations.

To search for properties that are eligible for HomePath financing, go to www.homepath.com.

Some California Specific Programs:

CalHFA (California Housing Finance Agency) FHA Loan Program:

This CalHFA FHA loan program is designed to enhance affordability and homeownership opportunities by offering a low, fixed interest rate that will not change during the entire loan term. This program is intended for first-time homebuyers who meet specific income and sales price requirements and who are purchasing a new or existing home anywhere in California.

How the Program Works - The CalHFA FHA offers financing up to 96.5% of the purchase price or appraised value whichever is less. To make owning a buyers' first home more affordable, down payment and closing cost assistance may be obtained when combining this CalHFA first mortgage with CHDAP (discussed later in this chapter) junior loan programs.

Program Elements-

- Must meet CalHFA Income limits. Find it here - http://goo.gl/pTZ2q
- Must meet CalHFA Sales Price limit for the County. Find it here - http://goo.gl/uBQS6
- Loan Amount capped at $417,000

California Homebuyers' down payment assistance program (CHDAP):

The CHDAP provides a deferred-payment junior loan – up to 3% of the purchase price, or appraised value, whichever is less – to qualified borrowers to be used for their down payment and/or closing costs. This junior loan may be combined with a CalHFA or non-CalHFA fixed rate, first mortgage loan. If combined with CalHFA FHA loan program, it offers potential First Time Home Buyers unique opportunity to buy a home with just 1% down payment.

California State Teachers Retirement System (CalSTRS) 80/17 program

The combined loan-to-value (LTV) ratio is 97% (80% LTV on the first mortgage and 17% LTV on the second mortgage).

A 3% down payment is required. A minimum of 1% must come from the borrower's own funds. The remainder may come from a gift from a relative where repayment is not required or a grant from a government agency or an employer - assisted housing program, which has been approved by Bank of America Home Loans.

Term – Both the first and second mortgages under the 80/17 Program have a 30 year term. The second mortgage has a five-year deferred payment structure.

Interest Rate - Both the first and corresponding second mortgage carry the same fixed interest rate.

Closing Costs - The closing costs and prepays can be paid from following sources:

- Borrower's own funds
- Seller contributions up to 3%
- Gift from relative

- Unsecured grant from a government agency or an employer - assisted housing program

The borrower (after closing) must have available cash reserves that equal at least two monthly mortgage payments. Funds from individual retirement accounts (IRA/Keogh accounts) and tax-favored retirement accounts (401k accounts) may be considered as cash reserves.

The Seller Buydown Strategy:

The beauty of the Seller BuyDown Strategy is its simplicity. It does not involve sophisticated mathematical equations, complicated explanations and it's not even a new concept. The Seller BuyDown Strategy is designed to be easy to understand and implement so that both the seller and the buyer can easily see that this truly is one of those rare win-win scenarios.

How It Works

The Seller Buy Down Strategy works by asking the seller to buy down the interest rate on the buyer's new home loan in lieu of asking for a purchase price reduction. By buying down the interest rate, the home buyer will see significantly lower payments than if they were to reduce the purchase price.

Here's a specific example of the benefits of the Seller Buy Down Strategy.

The Scenario

A seller is offering their home at a list price of $900,000. If a buyer were to make a full price offer with 20% down, this results in a monthly payment of $3,755.00 per month for a 30 Year Fixed loan at 4.75% rate.

The Offer with Seller Buy Down

Statistically speaking, most buyers will offer 3% below the list price on a property they are interested in. Rather than making a reduced price offer that will likely be overlooked, the buyer makes a full price offer and instead asks the seller to buy down their interest rate.

By using the same 3% difference to buy down their interest rate instead of reducing the purchase price, the buyer now gets a 4.25% rate and his/her monthly payment for 30 Year Fixed is $3541, a monthly saving of $214. But since this saving is permanent, over the term of the loan it translates to a whopping $77,040.

A True Win - Win Scenario

So instead of getting an instant $27,000 reduction in price, the seller buy down to reduce the interest rate saves the buyer an additional $50,040 ($77,040-$27,000) over the term of the loan. A seller would need to reduce the purchase price by almost $51,000 to match the monthly payment obtained using the Seller Buy Down Strategy. Also, for the buyer the 3% paid by the seller towards the buying down of the rate may be tax deductible in the year the home is purchased (please consult a tax professional to validate this).

Listing agents can use this strategy by marketing their property differently than most of the other agents who advertise the same boring "price reduced". Imagine the buzz you can create by advertising "Buy this $900,000 for the payment of a $849,000 house" or "This house qualifies for a 0.5% below market interest rate, ask me how". Note that by doing this, a seller can attract a larger pool of buyers since the reduced monthly payment would mean, potential buyers with slightly lesser income could qualify to buy the house too.

Again, we can't stress enough the importance of understanding the niche programs that are available in the market. With the depletion of financing choices, partnering up with a Loan Officer who truly is a professional and is an expert at these programs is more a necessity now than an option.

THE BUYERS AND SELLERS OF TOMORROW

If you plan to be in the Real Estate business for a long time, it's critical you understand the demographical changes that the country and more importantly your neighbourhood is going through. Below we present some of the biggest demographics that will shape up the future real estate market of the country. These are the people who would be buying and selling real estate in the future, are you geared to market to them?

Older Baby Boomers (Age 55-64): This segment constitutes about 26 million citizens who are stuck in their suburban properties because of the real estate bust, which has put them underwater i.e. they owe more on their mortgage than the property is worth. It is expected that older baby boomers who can sell their homes aren't necessarily following the road maps of previous generations. They are likely to move closer to their children and grand children instead of flocking to the retirement communities.

As they are healthier than their parents' generation, the older baby boomers will likely defer transitioning into retirement communities for at least a decade, thereby limiting demand for such facilities. They will instead prefer to purchase condominiums in the 'mixed-age and mixed-use communities' of more urbanized settings. Walkable, urbanized suburban town centres will see an influx of older baby boomers. Once the situation is conducive for boomers to sell their homes and buy condos, centres such as Bethesda, MD, and Reston, VA, as examples will thrive during the decade ahead.

Echo Boomers: According to the National Association of Housing Builders (NAHB), 83 million echo boomers will enter the housing market. Although they are expected to prefer the rental option to begin with considering the economic environment but will steadily move into the home ownership stage. Between 1981 and 1999, 81 million echo boomers were born compared to 78 million baby boomers that were born during 1946 to 1964. The sheer increase in number of these potential buyers coupled with rising aspirations will positively impact the residential real estate market. This generation is the largest generation in the US and comprises 25 percent of the population, just surpassing the baby boomers which represent slightly under 25 percent.

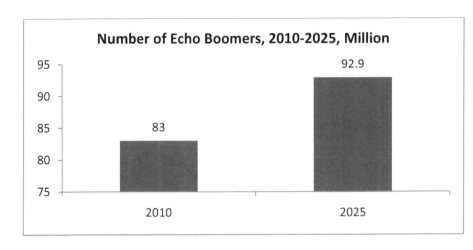

Under the Census Bureau's current estimate about immigration, the number of echo boomers will swell to 92.9 million by 2025. This highly diverse generation will give demand for apartments and smaller starter homes a lift over the next 15 years.

In the coming three to five years, housing in the US may see stability, which will be driven partially by the echo boomers with improved career prospects. Not only at one point they will get into home buying but until then they will keep pushing up the rentals which will benefit the existing homeowners and ultimately the home prices.

According to Urban Land Institute (ULI), home buying preferences of echo boomers include:

- Echo boomers do not prefer a home in the suburbs like their baby boomer parents did. They do not wish to limit themselves to major metros but are likely to be attracted to urban infill locations.
- Echo boomers want to live in culturally and ethnically diverse neighbourhoods.
- They increasingly gravitate to more affordable second tier and third tier cities if they are well-provided with enough recreational and entertainment amenities.
- This generation is environmentally conscious; hence they will prefer incorporated green building features.

As a result, the coming decades are likely to witness uptick in high-rise housing in relatively smaller cities to accommodate the housing needs of the echo boomers. Also, these trends indicate a strong potential in green housing market.

In a survey published by the ULI, the highest proportion of echo boomers presently rent or live with families but an overwhelming 70 percent expect to own a home by the time they touch thirties. 67 percent of all the respondents expect to own homes by 2015 while 73% percent of those at least 25 years of age and 78 percent of those aged 30 to 32 anticipate owning by 2015.

Immigration Trends: The drastic drop in household growth from 2005 to 2009 is partially attributed to marked drop in immigration. In this period, immigration, especially illegal, slowed sharply as a result of broad job losses. Between 2003 and 2009, immigrant and minority households contributed 74 percent of the net household growth in the country.

According to Harvard Housing Study, even if immigration comes to a halt today, past inflows and higher fertility rates will ensure that minorities and migrants will increasingly drive growth in housing demand. According to the Census Bureau's zero-immigration scenario, the minority share of the working-age population aged 25–64 would rise from 29 percent in 2000 to about 35 percent in 2020.

If immigration slows to about half the pace in the Census Bureau's current projections, and if headship rates by age and ethnicity remain at their 2008 levels, household growth during 2010–20 will come in at about 12.5 million. However, if immigration reaches the Census Bureau's estimate, household growth could climb closer to 14.8 million over the next 10 years.

Currently, there are approximately 40 million foreign-born people living legally or illegally in the United States, and this demographic is expected to grow in the coming years.

It is observed that immigrant populations tend to cluster together. These clusters are traditionally located in central cities but have started to move to inner suburbs over the last two decades. Housing demand from immigrants may one day flow to the larger suburban homes that are expected to face downward pricing pressure in the coming years. Such homes are attractive options for larger immigrant families.

Females in Workforce: Irrespective of the recession and the property price decline, the role of single female buyers has been expanding in the recent years and stood at 20 percent in 2010. This figure is more than double the number for single men. Growth in this segment of buyers is likely to contribute in keeping the real estate market buoyant in the coming years. Professional realtors are gearing up to assess needs of women homeowners and will get rewarded in the coming years for investing their time, energy and money in support of women homeownership.

Headship Rates: Defined as the propensity to form a household and determined by dividing the number of households by the region's population, the Headship Rate typically rises with age. Headship Rates among young adults declined in the late 2000s as a result of soaring unemployment in that age group.

However, headship rate is not likely to remain depressed for long because of dramatic improvements in affordability for first time buyers who have jobs. Even if immigration falls to half the Census Bureau's currently projected rate, household growth will still average about 1.25 million annually. Such a low estimate puts household growth in the next 10 years on par with the pace in 1995–2005.

A low-immigration scenario and assuming headship rates hold constant at 2008 levels, overall housing demand—including for second homes and replacement of older housing lost from the stock—should support more than 17 million new home completions and manufactured home placements between 2010 and 2020.

The US Census Bureau predicts the population to increase by 100 million during the next 30 years which translates into more than 3 million a year. This will necessarily boost overall demand for real estate and ultimately absorb excess housing inventory and propel greater demand for apartments.

Household Projections – Low Immigration Scenario (2010)

Age	Married Without Children	Partnered Without Children	Married With Children	Partnered With Children	Single Person	Single Parent Alone	Single Parent with Other Non-Partner Adults	Other	Total
15-19	27,009	76,472	29,797	35,637	1,40,035	32,477	33,625	5,01,847	8,76,899
20-24	5,10,148	5,48,884	6,89,188	3,32,781	14,66,510	4,87,926	1,58,168	14,69,545	56,63,150
25-29	13,16,644	6,80,970	24,13,753	4,67,889	21,66,880	9,90,640	1,87,329	11,51,805	93,75,909
30-34	12,19,764	3,81,669	42,33,465	3,47,929	17,57,696	12,42,717	2,25,608	6,45,047	1,00,53,894
35-39	9,49,435	2,67,788	51,83,796	2,97,141	16,39,424	11,84,423	3,81,686	5,02,272	1,04,05,967
40-44	14,01,758	3,42,213	51,13,884	2,20,616	19,65,927	10,53,709	4,95,371	7,29,919	1,13,23,397
45-49	28,81,088	3,77,569	41,09,106	1,37,964	25,83,194	7,64,476	4,07,737	11,24,896	1,23,86,031
50-54	47,11,104	3,37,782	22,47,202	52,229	29,48,227	3,65,772	2,36,037	13,15,275	1,22,13,628
55-59	55,84,261	2,68,208	8,05,225	12,953	31,22,592	1,38,863	81,714	12,20,347	1,12,34,163
60-64	52,83,346	1,96,635	2,72,859	7,695	31,02,965	40,548	24,485	9,67,020	98,95,554
65-69	40,17,787	1,04,069	94,170	1,625	25,98,807	23,955	19,604	7,41,847	76,01,865
70-74	26,70,502	54,296	46,151	2,146	21,98,613	12,527	8,237	5,47,563	55,40,036
75+	38,68,288	75,669	33,765	448	66,93,716	13,691	5,838	12,73,990	1,19,65,405
Total	3,44,41,134	37,12,225	2,52,72,364	19,17,055	3,23,84,585	63,51,725	22,65,438	1,21,91,372	11,85,35,898

Household Projections – Low Immigration Scenario (2015)

Age	Married Without Children	Partnered Without Children	Married With Children	Partnered With Children	Single Person	Single Parent Alone	Single Parent with Other Non-Partner Adults	Other	Total
15-19	26,353	72,605	29,410	34,824	1,31,870	30,446	32,213	4,85,577	8,43,298
20-24	5,06,193	5,40,108	7,06,780	3,37,198	14,49,445	4,96,373	1,62,522	14,76,796	56,75,416
25-29	13,37,281	6,92,263	24,69,053	4,80,470	22,13,900	10,31,608	1,94,509	11,78,007	95,97,091
30-34	13,06,085	4,09,187	45,01,792	3,70,606	18,89,181	13,31,694	2,39,690	6,84,048	1,07,32,282
35-39	9,57,131	2,69,253	52,50,678	3,03,014	16,61,366	12,14,098	3,95,691	5,14,646	1,05,65,877
40-44	13,28,860	3,21,372	49,21,979	2,16,520	18,62,250	10,17,739	4,95,293	7,18,943	1,08,82,956
45-49	26,15,024	3,43,498	37,99,039	1,30,075	23,45,971	7,07,627	3,86,382	10,55,907	1,13,83,524
50-54	47,03,861	3,37,612	22,74,008	54,145	29,51,160	3,69,977	2,44,941	13,42,609	1,22,78,312
55-59	61,34,441	2,94,648	9,02,675	14,745	34,53,477	1,56,013	94,583	13,81,551	1,24,32,132
60-64	58,76,834	2,19,530	3,13,925	9,160	34,79,334	47,348	28,245	11,11,602	1,10,85,977
65-69	51,46,487	1,33,823	1,23,437	2,099	33,43,040	31,178	26,094	9,69,503	97,75,661
70-74	32,27,870	65,613	56,688	2,592	26,51,368	14,895	10,042	6,62,440	66,91,507
75+	40,72,233	80,237	37,438	462	70,23,797	14,920	6,698	13,60,721	1,25,96,507
Total	3,72,38,655	37,79,750	2,53,86,901	19,55,911	3,44,56,158	64,63,916	23,16,902	1,29,42,350	12,45,40,541

Household Projections – High Immigration Scenario (2010)

Age	Married Without Children	Partnered Without Children	Married With Children	Partnered With Children	Single Person	Single Parent Alone	Single Parent with Other Non-Partner Adults	Other	Total
15-19	27,817	77,833	30,800	36,626	1,42,314	33,149	34,556	5,14,753	8,97,848
20-24	5,19,292	5,56,707	7,08,674	3,40,483	14,88,002	4,97,661	1,62,148	15,00,387	57,73,354
25-29	13,39,016	6,91,500	24,66,992	4,78,562	22,01,839	10,09,809	1,92,239	11,80,137	95,60,094
30-34	12,40,523	3,87,636	43,11,973	3,54,100	17,85,874	12,64,493	2,30,274	6,59,191	1,02,34,064
35-39	9,59,985	2,70,339	52,46,334	3,00,688	16,57,434	11,97,934	3,86,949	5,09,369	1,05,29,031
40-44	14,11,857	3,44,354	51,56,853	2,22,499	19,79,473	10,61,705	5,00,091	7,36,336	1,14,13,168
45-49	28,94,060	3,79,253	41,32,791	1,38,739	25,94,575	7,68,247	4,10,056	11,31,339	1,24,49,061
50-54	47,26,586	3,38,799	22,57,077	52,484	29,57,628	3,67,102	2,37,132	13,20,437	1,22,57,246
55-59	56,02,995	2,68,954	8,09,245	13,022	31,32,256	1,39,381	82,243	12,25,907	1,12,74,002
60-64	53,01,864	1,97,294	2,74,561	7,752	31,12,888	40,750	24,578	9,71,789	99,31,476
65-69	40,32,169	1,04,488	94,883	1,634	26,07,962	24,057	19,776	7,46,041	76,31,010
70-74	26,75,779	54,404	46,457	2,160	22,03,232	12,559	8,294	5,49,419	55,52,303
75+	38,71,259	75,743	33,858	448	66,97,780	13,717	5,859	12,75,531	1,19,74,195
Total	3,46,03,201	37,47,304	2,55,70,498	19,49,197	3,25,61,257	64,30,565	22,94,196	1,23,20,636	11,94,76,853

Household Projections – High Immigration Scenario (2015)

Age	Married Without Children	Partnered Without Children	Married With Children	Partnered With Children	Single Person	Single Parent Alone	Single Parent with Other Non-Partner Adults	Other	Total
15-19	28,017	75,390	31,473	36,859	1,36,534	31,824	34,125	5,12,128	8,86,350
20-24	5,24,873	5,56,030	7,46,785	3,52,982	14,93,244	5,16,293	1,70,687	15,40,023	59,00,917
25-29	13,82,872	7,13,660	25,77,993	5,02,341	22,85,122	10,70,814	2,04,598	12,36,219	99,73,621
30-34	13,48,348	4,21,297	46,61,988	3,83,184	19,46,471	13,76,129	2,49,252	7,13,063	1,10,99,733
35-39	9,78,600	2,74,413	53,78,280	3,10,248	16,98,016	12,41,633	4,06,481	5,29,200	1,08,16,870
40-44	13,49,398	3,25,704	50,09,785	2,20,371	18,89,769	10,34,042	5,04,984	7,32,088	1,10,66,139
45-49	26,41,440	3,46,927	38,47,582	1,31,663	23,69,145	7,15,329	3,91,138	10,69,122	1,15,12,347
50-54	47,35,669	3,39,699	22,94,386	54,673	29,70,466	3,72,713	2,47,200	13,53,237	1,23,68,042
55-59	61,72,954	2,96,175	9,10,979	14,886	34,73,317	1,57,079	95,678	13,93,023	1,25,14,091
60-64	59,14,939	2,20,884	3,17,446	9,276	34,99,721	47,764	28,436	11,21,450	1,11,59,915
65-69	51,76,066	1,34,686	1,24,913	2,117	33,61,855	31,389	26,451	9,78,169	98,35,646
70-74	32,38,788	65,835	57,322	2,620	26,60,913	14,962	10,159	6,66,282	67,16,881
75+	40,78,360	80,389	37,629	462	70,32,148	14,973	6,743	13,63,899	1,26,14,604
Total	3,75,70,322	38,51,089	2,59,96,561	20,21,682	3,48,16,722	66,24,943	23,75,933	1,32,07,905	12,64,65,156

Major Markets in 2011 and Beyond

PricewaterhouseCoopers conducted a survey to determine emerging trends in the US real estate. The study throws the following insights about the future of major real estate markets in the US.

Washington DC: Being the capital of the country, the city is home to the government which never downsizes. Lobbyists and consultants frequent the city to influence and participate in the policy making. Such activities support its property market and attract investors. The values have remained within 10 percent of the peak in the city.

New York City: Troubled Assets Relief Program (TARP) and Fed funds directed at banks helped markets with financial services businesses and curbed job cuts, benefiting New York City.

San Francisco: The City by the Bay offers investors market-bottom buying opportunities particularly in apartments. Economically, the city has performed better than southern California. Technology and life sciences industries flourish enabled by the top universities (Stanford and Berkeley). However, San Jose struggles with oversupply of condos.

Boston: The city ranks high on livability, controlled development, and a highly educated labor force, but lacks economic vibrancy. Boston is likely to offer steady core returns with sustained buyer interest and will provide decent appreciation potential in the future.

Seattle: The city benefits from high immigration in the area and has gained 160,000 residents since the recession. The technology firms in the area are still right-sizing and the city could face further economic downside. Housing localities closer to the core of the city still hold potential.

Houston: The world oil and gas business capital's vacancy rates stand below the national average. The city prepares for the strategic port expansion to augment shipping traffic from the Pacific through the expanded Panama Canal, scheduled for 2014. Population inflows keep the housing occupancy stable and create more demand for real estate.

Los Angeles: The survey interviewees consider California struggling from high taxes and anti-business environment. But they do realize the tantalizing opportunity it presents for investors to invest in real estate at never before throwaway prices. The possibility of southern California to bounce back faster than most markets is quite a likely scenario. In addition, it also holds the coveted status of gateway to

Latin America and the Pacific Rim which further highlights its significance to the state's economy.

San Diego: The city has a similar story as Los Angeles except for the gateway status. The city boasts of the best climate in the country but lags in large scale economic activity. Public companies buy relatively cheap land here and wait for an eventual bounce back.

Denver: The city has strengthened its public transport infrastructure to position itself for the 21st century. It has one of the nation's most modern airports, an attractive Rocky Mountain backdrop, relatively low business taxes, and a broad-based economy anchored by oil and gas, alternative energy, and defense companies. The office market has stabilised and should expect the residential apartments to fill up soon.

Dallas: The recession in the city was well in control but current prospects are subdued. The city typically has faced strong demand and even larger supply owing to the presence of most developers in the continent. Apartment builders in the city can potentially do well but existing investors face a tough time as they continuously face new competition.

Chicago: The city is an important interior gateway but is hard hit by the dwindling mid west industries in the mid west and an unfavourable region wide demographics. Most residential construction has halted and there is oversupply in the retail and the hotel space.

Philadelphia: The hope remains for a super fast train that could link the city to Manhattan and boost the real estate. Overall, the institutional investors are not excited about the city's near term future.

Miami: Interviewees express confidence in the city and southern Florida. It is a popular destination for visitors and baby boomer retirees apart from being a global commercial hub. At present, the housing is extremely down but apartments are holding ground. The city is expected to build up and urbanize when expected population growth resumes.

Atlanta: An ideal metro with favourable demographic movement towards the infill districts of the city. The city developed the critical mass for growth and the government had recently invested to address traffic issues. Unfortunately, the recession occurred at the wrong time and the city presently suffers from extreme over supply.

Phoenix: The city suffers from over supply and deep recession. Although property prices are rock bottom but are expected to go down further. The city struggles with other issues such as boycotts and immigrant labor that is left with no work.

MASTERING THE REO BUSINESS

Today you can't just spend hours working with home buyers and sellers listing or selling them a great home and then waiting years before they need your services again. And yet what is the alternative if you want regular business in your pipeline. Think REOs, short sales and investors.

Instead of buying or selling a home every 5-7 years investors buy one or two a year sometimes even more. By developing skills to serve clients who want to invest in real estate you'll position yourself for what we call full spectrum real estate—a model of regular clients with the added potential of the investor client enabling you to build a more consistent, profitable business model for yourself.

And since real estate often tends to move in the opposite direction of the stock market, it offers investors a way to diversify their investment portfolios and with the current valuation of many real estate markets (the lowest prices in years) investors can experience cash flow on a rental immediately and appreciation over time. In fact, today smart investors should have 5-10% (not counting their principal residence) in real estate.

The Investor Client

At the same time, working with investors takes a whole different mindset. Where a traditional buyer or seller will look first at location and amenities, investors look at the numbers. Thus, there are several critical areas of focus for investors and thus for you:

- Cash is king but if financing is necessary does your investor have the networking to tap into the lending market to make sure they can get funding or some extra cash to bring to the table

- You must be able to calculate an accurate income and expense analysis for investor clients. Will the upside potential come from increased cash flow or appreciation or from both and over what period of time?

- You must know the "right" market areas for investors—cheap does not equate to value or upside potential and in foreclosure and short sales markets not all the properties are desirable

- You have to build a stable of vendors who once the investor has purchased the property can do the necessary repairs or remodels quickly and cost effectively so that the property can start to produce income

- You must educate yourself on the different contracts for investors—for example an investor buying a short sale from an owner occupied seller has different mandates like the right of remission that allows the seller to come back for up to two years and repurchase the property. The special contract for this situation available through CAR forms speaks specifically to this situation, outlines the rights and rules of both the buyer and seller.

- You should be able to offer or provide property management services to the investors too

Just remember investors are looking to build wealth not just to buy or sell something.

Becoming an REO Real Estate Agent

As for becoming a REO agent will you be a listing agent or a buyer agent or both?

Becoming a REO listing real estate agent takes networking with banks and asset management companies that control the REO inventory. They usually like to work with a select group of agents in their various markets that know their system, that have the financial ability to upfront all the costs of getting the property on the market and have enough staff to handle the myriad of details (from getting pictures, handling tenants, turning on the utilities and keeping the property maintained etc.) that go with listing REO's beyond the normal listing process.

Listings are usually sent via e-mail and you have 24 hours to accept or reject them. You then have 24 hours to see if there are tenants in the property and make a recommendation as to what to do with them—evict them or offer cash for keys amount. Next is to do an inventory of what is in the property with suggestions for what to do with it, then turning on the utilities in your name and starting the clean up process by getting bids and hiring vendors. Next comes the pictures (they usually want 40-50) of each area inside and outside and your recommendations of what needs repairs or renovations. Then comes the bidding process for getting these repairs done—sometimes they will give you an amount to work with but sometimes each bid needs to be approved. As the property gets renovated and ready to be put on the market they will want your marketing plan including lots of comparables, specifics on pendings, recent sales, inventory, days of properties on the market, your marketing plans for the property etc. They will want weekly updates on market activity and full-blown monthly reports including activity and new market comps. Lastly will be the billing for reimbursement—each vendor should be put on a separate invoice with their bid and approved verification if that was necessary, then add before and after pictures, a copy of the check to the vendor, a 1099 from the vendor and any other documentation that is needed. Expect to bill the bank or asset management company monthly but also expect that it will take at least three months to get reimbursed. Also, be prepared to have funds of from $1,000 to 5,000 to upfront on each property.

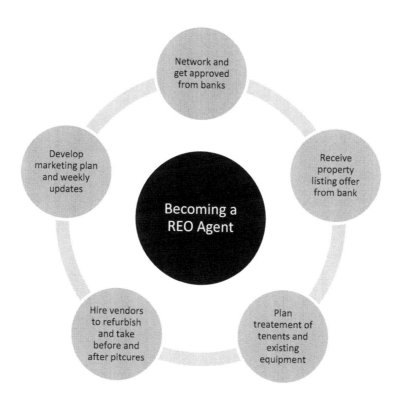

Becoming a REO Agent

- Network and get approved from banks
- Receive property listing offer from bank
- Plan treatement of tenents and existing equipment
- Hire vendors to refurbish and take before and after pitcures
- Develop marketing plan and weekly updates

If you are interested in becoming a REO real estate agent, contact the banks and ask for the departments that handle these properties. Send in an application and develop traction by initially conducting appraisals for them at no charge. This is the way to get on their list.

As a REO buyers real estate agent you need to have a realistic understanding with your clients of what it is going to take with respect to funding and price to win in the foreclosure and short sale markets. Just because these markets have been tagged "distressed", many buyers think that they can purchase these properties way below list price. Nothing could be further from the truth—especially in the "hot" foreclosure and short sales markets inventory is so low (often only 1-2 months) that properties go over the list price with multiple offers. Thus first and foremost, cash offers are king. Also, realizing that the list price is different than the bid price and the winning price is often the key to getting the property. Even more important than the list price in these hot markets is the number of offers—for each offer the bid price goes up by a factor of $1500 -$2000 per offer and thus the winning bid will be greater than the asking price.

You will often find short sales in the same market areas as foreclosures but they are different. Yes, short sales need bank approvals as do foreclosures in order to be sold but unlike in foreclosures, in short sales the sellers are still involved and have to sign off on the transaction. Short sales also involve more players—several banks, lien holders, delinquencies like late property taxes or unpaid homeowners dues. All of these must be handled, so short sales take more time (think 4-8 months) and involve the approval of multiple players not just the primary lien holder.

If you are listing a short sales make sure that the sellers also know that their credit will be affected for 3-5 years, their FICO score will fall by 75-100 points and there will probably be tax consequences if any of the money on the loan being forgiven was used to purchase anything other than the property or renovation of the property. Many short sellers think that because the Federal government passed a law in 2007 that allowed forgiveness of debt under short sales to be a non-taxable event that they are off the hook for any taxes due. Well, it depends—as we said as long as the loan was used for purchase of the property or renovation then there is no tax consequence. But if any of the money was used for example to purchase a car, pay off credit card debt etc… that portion will be taxed as income. Another little quirk of short sales, often banks will require a seller to sign an unsecured note for the amount the bank is forgiving or they will not approve the transaction.

So whether you want to develop a full-blown new real estate strategy or simply expand your business model there are many different kinds of clients out there eager to take your advice. From first time buyers, to the organic move up move around buyers and now to investors you have many new opportunities. You just have to think differently about real estate. Today it's more about the investment than the dream. So you need to educate them, show them how the asset real estate and not just the dream of real estate can build wealth for them with statistics and hard information. That is the way you will win in real estate today.

GENERATING BUSINESS ON THE WEB

Online marketing like any other marketing needs to serve one purpose – getting you more leads and clients. National Association of Realtors reported than in 2009 more than 90% of consumers searched online for homes for sale (see the chart) and the first thing that ~50% prospects did when they thought of buying a home was to go online.

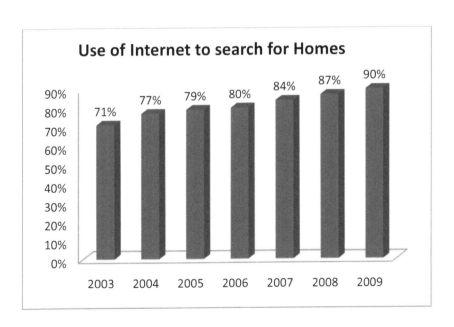

While prospects are frequenting several platforms like Blogs, Social Media sites like Facebook, Twitter and LinkedIn, Video sharing sites like YouTube (see the chart – source emarketer) to find and share information, most of the real estate agents are still stuck with having a plain vanilla website which was created long ago and since has barely been updated. Most of the experts are calling the shift in how consumers access information as the biggest shift since Industrial Revolution. Still, here we are, stuck with our dated websites that rarely work!

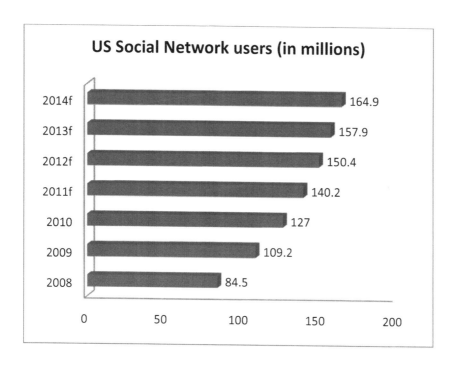

US Social Network users (in millions)

Year	Users
2014f	164.9
2013f	157.9
2012f	150.4
2011f	140.2
2010	127
2009	109.2
2008	84.5

Online marketing can be broken down into 3 stages – converting Suspects to Customers:

- Getting traffic to your site
- Capturing your visitor's information i.e. Getting leads from your traffic
- Following up with those clients till they are ready to use our services i.e. Converting leads into customers

Step 1: Getting traffic to your site

Just couple of years ago, if we had mentioned this, there was only one possible place you could have directed your traffic to – your website. Now you can possibly do this to multiple places. Some of the examples are:

- Your website
- Your blog
- Your Facebook personal profile or business page
- Your YouTube channel

However, trying to drive traffic to multiple sites all at once is not easy to achieve and hence not advisable. We instead recommend a "hub and spoke" model, where all the possible platforms are used to drive traffic to one site.

If you noticed, we suggest you should have your blog as the hub with all the spokes around it. You may be thinking what exactly a blog is and how is it different from a website that you most likely already have. Or more importantly, why *that* should be the hub? Here is the answer:

- Blogs can be quickly and easily updated at regular, short intervals, allowing for timely information and advice. All this without involving your webmaster or tech support.
- Blogs are a traffic magnet - Search engines love blogs because of their fresh and frequent new information.
- Blogs are interactive because people can leave comments and you can respond to them.
- Blogs are a trust builder - Studies show that people tend to trust information written on a blog more than on traditional websites.
- Blogs help you get more traffic and inbound links (see the chart, source - Hubspot).

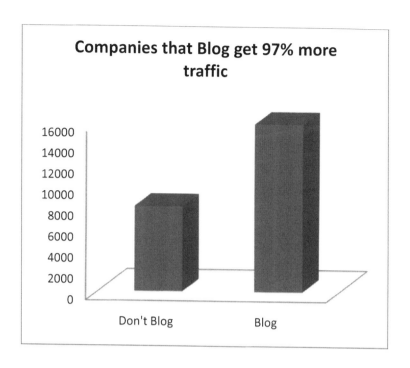

How to get started with Blogging:

Many blogging platforms or tools exist to help you quickly set up a blog site. Some of the more popular ones are blogger.com, typepad.com and wordpress.com. WordPress is the established leader with the most users. But whatever platform you pick, it's important that your blog not include the name of the platform in its web site address. For example ____.wordpress.com. We suggest you buy a domain name specifically for your blogs. The domain name should be based on the niche or Geography that you target and not your name e.g.

www.ForeclosureExpertInSanJose.com. This helps you rank higher for those Keywords on Google and other search engines. You can buy one relatively inexpensive ($8-$11/year) from sites like www.GoDaddy.com. After you have bought the domain name, contact their customer support so that you can host the website with them ($4-$6/month) and move the domain name to the Wordpress platform (free).

One of the other platforms for Real Estate Professionals is ActiveRain. It is the largest online gathering of real estate people in the word. At the time of writing this book they had ~ 200,000 members. You can write blogs for free to target other real estate professionals or can even publish it for consumers with a small monthly fee. This is where you can go to sign up with them - https://activerain.com/login.

Once you have the blog site up and running, you need to start publishing content on this site.

That brings us to 6 habits of highly effective content creation:

Content – The heart and the soul of a blog is content. Focusing on a certain niche is always recommended. This niche could be a market segment like First Time Home Buyers, Single women, Veterans etc. or could be a geographic area like San Jose, CA. You could even mix the two by writing contents only for First Time Home Buyers who want to buy a house in San Jose, CA. A new buzz word in Real Estate social media strategy is hyper-local blogging. Hyper-local blogs are also known as city or neighborhood blogs. Not only these kinds of blogs makes you a local expert in the eyes of visitors to your blog, but it's great even from the Search Engine Optimization (SEO) perspective, meaning your blog can rank higher in Google searches.

How Often – Blog two or three times a week. If you cannot come up with so many ideas at least write one blog a week. If you can't think of anything else, you can always write a weekly real estate market update for your local area. This can talk about the inventory levels, property prices etc.

Topic Ideas – Ideas for a Blog post is all around us. Anything that pertains to your niche and something that will interest your readers is an idea for a blog: How-to articles, analysis of a current industry trend, challenge and opportunities in this market, your new listing and even announcement of upcoming events. You can find such ideas from media, other industry blogs or your own experience. Sometimes you can simply give your readers a list of links to 5 other relevant articles that you have read or videos you've watched.

In addition to your own blog content, you can invite others to write on your blog. As a real estate agent, you can ask a mortgage professional or other affiliate partners to contribute some articles about their business. You can even invite your customers to write about their experience and how other prospects can learn from that experience. Guest articles lessen your content creation load and expose your readers to more ideas.

Blog Title – Spend some time on selecting the title of your article. You would want to make it as irresistible as possible so that your readers are tempted to read it. Numbered lists work very well, for example "7 things you must know before buying a foreclosure property", "5 ways to save thousands of dollars in remodelling cost". Think about why headlines in magazines grab our attention!

Do not oversell – Always remember the purpose of blogs is educational in nature. One of the biggest reasons Blogs fail is because authors are more concerned about selling their products and services than providing unbiased information.

Engage with comments section – When you begin Blogging you may want to turn off the comments section. It could be a little disconcerting to think others can openly comment on our thoughts. But with experience you would realize it is in your best interest to encourage readers to leave comments, whether they agree with you or not. It gives you an opportunity to interact with them. Engaging them in a conversation will attract a lot more qualified prospects.

Mix it up – All your content does not have to be in print. Mix them up with some videos. Keep it short 2-3 minutes. It can be just PowerPoint slides converted to video or YouTube videos embedded in your blog post. Videos is quickly becoming the preferred way of getting information (see chart on the next page, Source -emarketer).

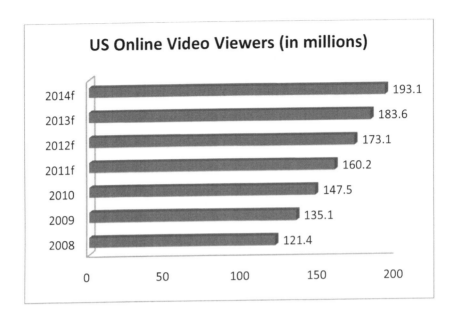

One of the easiest tools to create stunning videos for your listings and other business needs is Animoto. Go to http://animoto.com/pricing to sign up for a free basic account to get familiar with the software. Once you become comfortable, plan on signing up for Pro account that allows unlimited high definition videos of unlimited length and other cool features. See Animoto Pro in action in this video http://goo.gl/bdOFu

If you would rather simply capture information on the computer screen with your voice over, try a screen casting software like Jing (get the free version at http://www.techsmith.com/jing/free/ or the pro version at http://www.techsmith.com/jing/pro/) or for more advanced features and longer videos try Camtasia (get the free trial version at http://www.techsmith.com/camtasia/). If you are trying screen casting make sure you invest in a good microphone.

And if you need to shoot yourself or something else, you can use the following easy to use and carry video cameras (in order of preference):

- Kodak Zi8
- Flip
- Your smart phones – Droid or iPhone

The first 2 in the list are almost identical, but the Kodak Zi8 scores on having better audio quality when recording. The entry level models for both video cameras are now available for less than $100.00 on Amazon.

Spreading the word about your blog posts:

- Share your post on Social Media Platforms like Facebook, Twitter and LinkedIn
- Add your Blog website address to your E-mail signature
- Include a Share it button and Subscribe option on your blog

- Participate on consumer forums like Zillow, and guide the prospects to your blog post if you think it helps answers their question
- Include your website address in all your offline and online marketing

Creating optimized local accounts:

A lot of searches are moving local both on computers and mobile phones. Hence it's important that you get found when potential customers are looking for you. The top 3 sites where you should register your business are:

Google Places – With a free Google Places account, you can easily get found on Google when people are searching for a Real Estate agent in your area and also engage visitors with photos, offers and reviews. You can go here to sign up for a free account –

http://places.google.com/business.

Businesses on Google places always rank on page 1 for local listings. So having a profile on Google is probably the easiest way to get found on Google. It's like getting your business advertised for free on Google. Top tips (directly from Google) to get your business ranked higher with Google Places account:

Business Name: Represent your business exactly as it appears in the offline world.

- Do not include marketing taglines in your business name.
- Do not include phone numbers or URLs in the business name field, unless they are part of your business name.
- Do not attempt to manipulate search results by adding extraneous keywords or a description of your business in the business name field.

Business Location: Use a precise, accurate address to describe your business location.

- Do not create listings at locations where the business does not physically exist. P.O. Boxes are not considered accurate physical locations. Listings submitted with P.O. Box addresses will be removed.
- Use the precise address for the business in place of broad city names or cross-streets.
- Do not create more than one listing for each business location, either in a single account or multiple accounts.

- Businesses that operate in a service area, as opposed to a single location, should not create a listing for every city they service. Businesses that operate in a service area should create one listing for the central office or location and designate service areas.
- Do not include information in address lines that does not pertain your business's physical location (e.g. URLs, keywords).

Website & Phone: Provide a phone number that connects to your individual business location as directly as possible, and provide one website that represents your individual business location.

- Use a local phone number instead of a call center number whenever possible.
- Do not provide phone numbers or URLs that redirect or "refer" users to landing pages or phone numbers other than those of the actual business.

Yelp – Get your satisfied clients to post reviews for you and get found on the largest online consumer review site in the world. You can create a free business account at -

https://biz.yelp.com/. Here's what you will see on your Yelp for Business Owners account:

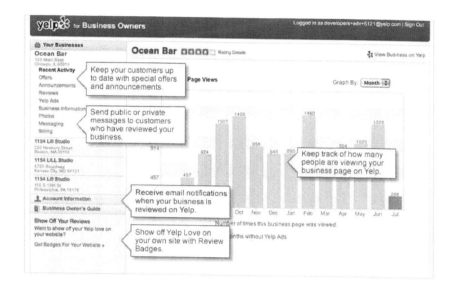

Also, don't forget to create Offers & Announcements to tell potential customers about upcoming events, special offers and more.

Yahoo! Local – Potential customers from every area visit Yahoo! Local every day. You can either get a basic listing for free or pay a small monthly amount for an "enhanced" listing. To sign up go to - http://listings.local.yahoo.com/.

To compare the difference between free and enhanced plan ($9/95/month) go to -

http://listings.local.yahoo.com/comp.php.

Step 2: Getting leads from your traffic

Once you get traffic to your site, your aim should be to convert some of that traffic into leads. In Online Marketing terms, these are the people who "opt-in" to receive future communications from you. This can be achieved by providing something of value in exchange of which they would be willing to provide their information. A note about sign-up forms – the less information you ask for, the more likely people would be willing to provide their information. So if you do not plan to call the leads that you generate from online marketing, do not bother asking for their phone numbers. If you have an effective follow up system (discussed later in this chapter), usually just getting the name and email address should be good enough.

Some of the ways you are able to capture potential buyers and sellers' personal information is detailed below:

Subscribe to future posts – If the visitors to your blog really like your posted content, they would be interested in signing up to receive future posts via email. You can have an option on your website for visitors to subscribe via email or RSS (Really Simple Syndication). Read more about RSS here http://en.wikipedia.org/wiki/RSS.

Free give-aways – As a Real Estate agent you can provide a lot of valuable information as free give-aways on your website in exchange for some basic information. Some of the examples are:

- Find out what is your home worth
- Download a free Home Buying guide
- Download a free Relocation guide
- Register for free Home Buyer Seminars/Webinars
- Get weekly/monthly Real Estate Market trends
- Get a complimentary mortgage pre-approval or rate quote (you can partner up with your Loan Officer to offer this)

IDX - IDX is a type of data feed provided by your MLS membership. In some cases your MLS may require that you pay for access to this data feed. This data feed typically (but not always) mirrors the data available on your

MLS's website. If your MLS provides access to this data feed, you may use that access to promote ALL listings on your website, not just your featured listings.

IDX is one of the top ways to capture leads online. It not only provides the convenience to the visitors of your website to search for homes, it also allows them to save their preference and even receive automatic emails when a new property is listed that matches their preference. And most importantly, it requires registration by the potential buyers in exchange for all this self –service home search automation tools. Most of the Real Estate agents who generate lot of business via online marketing quote IDX as their #1 lead capture tool. Not all IDX companies provide IDX tools for all counties. Check with these websites to find out who offers the tools that best suits your business goals:

www.PropertyMinder.com

www.DiverseSolutions.com

www.IDXBroker.com

Connect on Social Media Platforms - You should encourage visitors to your website to also connect with you on Social Media Platforms like Facebook, Twitter and LinkedIn. If you are providing valuable information on these platforms, not only you will remain on top of mind of your prospects/clients, it will quickly position you as an expert. If you are not present on these platforms, consider becoming a part of these communities ASAP. Here's why - Recommendations from personal acquaintances or opinions posted by consumers online are the most trusted forms of advertising, according to the Nielsen Global Online Consumer Survey (see the chart). Ninety percent or consumers surveyed noted that they trust recommendations from people they know, while 70 percent trusted consumer opinions posted online. Note that the survey was done in April 2009; most likely those numbers would have gone up since.

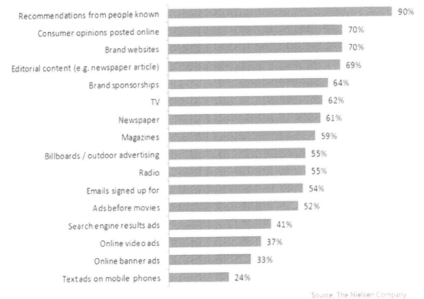

Have some degree of trust* in the following forms of advertising
April 2009

Recommendations from people known	90%
Consumer opinions posted online	70%
Brand websites	70%
Editorial content (e.g. newspaper article)	69%
Brand sponsorships	64%
TV	62%
Newspaper	61%
Magazines	59%
Billboards / outdoor advertising	55%
Radio	55%
Emails signed up for	54%
Ads before movies	52%
Search engine results ads	41%
Online video ads	37%
Online banner ads	33%
Text ads on mobile phones	24%

Source: The Nielsen Company

*E.g. 90 percent of respondents trusted "completely" or "somewhat" recommendations from people they know

Make sure you follow the golden rules of participating on Social Media. The 10 Do's and Don'ts of Social Media-

1. Give something of value - all the time.
2. Remain professional if you are using this as a business tool.
3. Have fun once in a while.
4. Stay away from Political, Religious and Social issues which could be offensive.
5. Stop selling, start engaging.

6. Owning your database has never been easier, if you do it right.

7. Create a realistic communications strategy – and stick to it.

8. Develop a style and personality.

9. Be honest.

10. Don't ignore feedback – positive or negative.

Step 3: Converting your leads into clients

Autoresponders

The autoresponder as the name suggests is a message that goes out immediately (and automatically) when someone subscribes to your list. It's also often referred to as the welcome message of a campaign. The autoresponder message could be just the welcome message or a series of messages auto-programmed to go at certain time intervals.

Why Do I Need One?

It's important to have something sent to subscribers when they sign up, regardless of whether you plan to follow up with a whole sequence of messages or only scheduled newsletters.

A subscriber's interest is often at a very high point when they sign up for your email campaign. Therefore, skipping this step or giving little attention can result in a missed opportunity for your business.

What Should I Write?

There are a few key things you should communicate to subscribers in your welcome message:

Confirm that they signed up for your email campaign: This message is part transactional. By confirming this for the subscriber, you make them comfortable in feeling that they've taken the steps necessary to receive the messages they want from you.

Thank them for signing up: Be polite! It goes a long way. Express to your subscribers that you're truly grateful to have an opportunity to share your expertise and provide useful information for them.

If you offered a free bonus for signing up, deliver it: Provide any free content promptly. Offering free, useful material exhibits the fact that you have the subscriber's interests in mind more than just their money, making them more likely to do business with you.

Introduce yourself as an approachable, expert resource: Your business' advantage has a lot to do with the personal service you offer, along with your experience. By making yourself available to subscribers should they have any questions, you increase their confidence in your service.

Remind them how they will benefit from your future messages: Are you sending a series of helpful tips, a newsletter, new listings? All of the above? Remind subscribers of why they should be on the lookout for your next message and beyond.

What Else Should I Add?

Remember that an effective campaign will continually build a relationship with subscribers, so you don't need to write it all in one message. Instead, get something in your first message, and then work on a second, third, and so on when you have some time.

Try www.Aweber.com to find out how you can include autoresponders into your online marketing mix.

Email Marketing

Here are the 6 reasons why you should consider email marketing

1. Email marketing has a broad reach

It's tough to find anyone who doesn't have at least one email address, which means you can reach out to your entire customer and prospect base. Just be sure to get their permission first by asking if you can add them to your mailing list.

2. Email marketing is targeted

Most forms of advertising are based on the idea that if you hit thousands of people with your message, even though it may mean nothing to most of them, a few are likely to respond.

Email marketing is based on the idea of sending the right message directly to the right people based on their preferences, local market conditions, and other factors.

You can build a master list and then segment it by geographic location, marital status, gender, age, income, time of year, etc. Doing so eliminates a lot of the guesswork that makes other forms of marketing so inefficient.

3. Email marketing provides data

If you're using an email marketing application or service designed for small business operators like www.MailChimp.com or www.ConstantContact.com, you can run reports that show which emails or messages worked and which didn't, so you can improve your next campaign.

You can even run split tests, sending one offer or message to half your list and a different one to the other half, so you can get a better feel for exactly what makes customers and prospects buy from you.

4. Email marketing allows you to engage

As a Real Estate agent, your real goal is to build a relationship with a broader base of prospects so they think of you whenever it's time to for them to buy or sell.

Email marketing allows you to do that by providing them tips, updates on market trends and special give-aways on a regular basis. It's a great way to engage them—and keep them engaged.

5. Email marketing has a low cost of entry

Most forms of advertising or marketing require a big up-front investment before you see any results. That can get expensive for a Real Estate Agent like you who is trying to keep expenses down.

Email marketing has very little up-front cost, allowing you to market effectively without having to stop your core business work for long periods to get it done.

6. Email marketing works

According to the DMA's research, email marketing generated a return on investment (ROI) of $43.62 for every dollar spent on it in 2009. You're unlikely to find that kind of ROI from any other form of marketing or advertising—the best reason of all to launch an email-marketing campaign.

Events

One of the other ways in which you can remain in touch with your prospects is by conducting educational events. You can do these as in-person seminars or webinars. The latter offers convenience and ease of execution but takes away face-to-face interaction which a live seminar can offer. Consider, partnering up with your lending and other affiliate partners for these events, so that you can leverage their database and expertise. If you are just getting started with webinars, you can get a free trial to conduct webinars at www.GoToMeeting.com.

Again, if you could execute all three facets of online marketing i.e. Getting visitors to your site, Capturing their information and Following up with them, then very soon you would be able to generate a lot of business from web.

A lot of what we discussed in terms of Online Marketing (more specifically blogging) can be seen in action at www.LendingExpertBlog.com.

CREATING THE MEGA BRAND CALLED – YOU!

"Products and services are systems created in the workplace but brands are images created in the mind"

That is why brand building is so important because it is a visual promise that your clients believe in. Then, because of that you create trust and emotional attachment, build awareness, prompt client selections and create more business for yourself.

Branding is a circular sphere:

First you create an image of yourself and your service or product in the clients mind.

Second you promise what you say you can do.

Third you present the service—what it is, how it will be used, the benefits to the client and how your service stands out from the competition.

Fourth, with superior follow through you leave a lasting image in the mind of your client.

Most people rush to the third step and thus fail to build their brand with the client. Brands are built around 4 keys:

- Service differentiation
- Relevance—the client sees it and knows it
- Esteem—quality
- Knowledge—information that matters not just data

So how do you build your brand?

It is all about the marketing you do of yourself—that investment in your business about you not just the advertising of the properties you sell.

Think PR—events, meetings, newsletters, and sponsorships.

Think Promotions.

Thinks mailings—e-mails and direct mail.

Think a mixture of your marketing with advertising—newspaper, magazines, radio and TV, brochures, printed material.

Think the Internet—Google, Yahoo, Facebook, Twitter, craigslist, realtor.com, blogs.

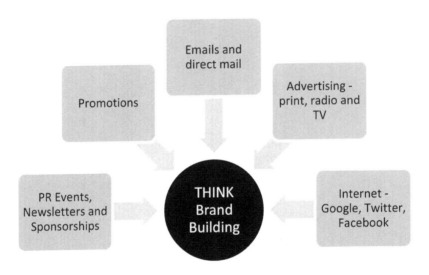

Here are 10 truths about branding:

- They need positioning—one consistent image done over and over so it stays in the client's mind
- It is a promise kept—you have to deliver what you promise

- It happens from your mission statement and your goals then outward into your marketing
- It must have a consistent theme
- You power the brand and then the power of your brand follows you
- Brands live in your client's mind or it is not a brand
- Branding starts and ends with the image your clients have of you
- Brands need to be updated on an ongoing basis
- Brands are one of your most valuable assets

Here are 10 Myths about Branding

- Branding is all you need—no it is a very important piece of how your clients see you but it has to be followed up with hard work and unexpected service excellence.
- I don't need a brand—yes you do .If you do not have one, your clients see you as a real estate agent among thousands; those with a brand stand out from the crowd. Think Apple versus computers, think Coke versus colas, think Nike versus tennis shoes.
- Your brand can say many things—no your brand has to give off one consistent message about who you are.

- The brand will do all the differentiating I need—no you have to be able to back up the brand with a service that you can define that sets you apart from your competition.
- Branding is easy to create and easy to protect—no it takes time to build and you need to protect it.
- Believing that the brand is more important than what you do—the brand should create an image of what you do in the client's mind. It is not separate from what you do.
- Thinking that if you have a brand it is enough—having a brand means you have to do more not less because what you have in your brand that someone who doesn't have one is missing—you have created an image, a memory in your client's mind of who you are and what you do.
- Changing the look of a brand keeps it fresh—no *tweaking* the look of the brand keeps it fresh.

Some great brands to think about:

- ❖ Coca Cola
- ❖ Microsoft
- ❖ General Electric
- ❖ Google
- ❖ Toyota
- ❖ Disney

- ❖ McDonalds
- ❖ Ralph Lauren
- ❖ BMW
- ❖ Louis Vuitton
- ❖ Wal-Mart
- ❖ Hewlett Packard
- ❖ Apple

What makes them so special?

- They are simple yet great
- They send an instant compelling message
- They promise and deliver
- They have distinctive products or services
- They put forth a consistent message
- They put forth one message over and over again—for Disney it's the place to go for family entertainment, for Coke it's the pause that refreshes, for Apple it's the coolest tech products
- They leave their customers with a "wow" experience
- They adapt and adjust to the times
- They emote passion

So what's your brand?

- What is the image that you create in your client's minds?

- Do your clients relate to you on an emotional level?
- Can your clients see how you are different from your competition?
- Does your brand talk to the needs of your clients as a picture in their minds?
- What does your brand do better than anybody else's?
- Does your brand include a theme or tag line?

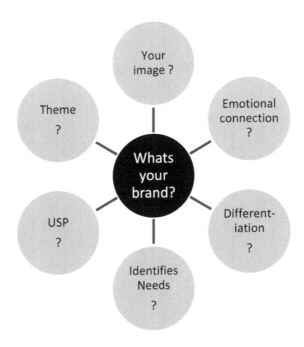

Some examples of branding that work:

- Jane Brown, a realtor with a different point of view—yours

- Bob Woods, a realtor selling the best properties in town

So, if you have a brand, enhance it, market it and if not go create one.

HOPE IS NOT A STRATEGY, PLANNING IS

Successful businesses follow more a circular strategy than a linear one. What we mean by that is successful businesses Plan, Execute, Measure and then go back to planning based on the measured results.

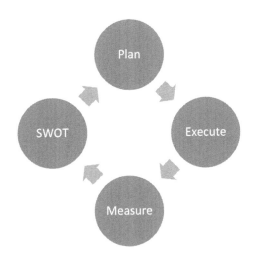

Let's talk about each of these steps.

Plan – We are amazed at how many agents run their businesses without proper planning and goal-setting. So if you are one of those who is not sure about the benefits of planning. Here they are:

- Planning promotes focus.
- Planning provides performance standards.
- Planning coordinates efforts and activities.
- Planning reveals obstacles and roadblocks.
- Planning stimulates insights and ideas.
- Planning saves you 10 to 1 in execution.

Where does planning begin?

SWOT analysis: Start by doing a Strength, Weakness, Opportunities and Threat (SWOT) analysis for you and your business. The technique is credited to Albert Humphrey, who led a convention at Stanford University in the 1960s and 1970s using data from Fortune 500 companies.

A SWOT analysis should be incorporated *into* the strategic planning model.

Strengths: characteristics of the business or team that give it an advantage over others in the industry.

Weaknesses: characteristics that place the business at a disadvantage relative to others.

Opportunities: *external* chances to make greater sales or profits in the environment.

Threats: *external* elements in the environment that could cause trouble for the business.

Identification of SWOTs is essential because subsequent steps in the process of planning for achievement of the selected objective(s) may be derived from the SWOTs.

Finding a Niche: We all know the phrase "Jack of all, Master of none". The Real Estate business has become way too demanding to be a "Jack", you *have* to be a "Master" now.

What *is a niche?* It's a subset of the overall market. Focusing your marketing on a niche means addressing a need that isn't being addressed by many people if any at all. Completing the SWOT analysis will help you identify your core competence which will enable you to find your niche. You can decide on a niche based on several different factors like:

- Niche by geography
- Niche by demography
- Niche by transaction type
- Niche by buyer type
- Niche by property type, etc.

Why serve a niche market? There are a number of reasons why you can be more profitable in a niche market:

- *Targeted marketing* - You can more readily identify target customers for what you sell and reach them through marketing. You'll also be more "findable" on the Web by customers who want what you offer.
- *Competition* – Most of the agents are spreading their marketing dollars over a broader market and aren't focusing on the customers you can serve.
- *Expertise* - You can gain a reputation as being more knowledgeable about your service area than other "general" agents, attracting a special group of customers.

It's better to dominate a small market (niche) and capture most of its business than being "just another player" in a big market and getting little to no business.

Now that I have hopefully convinced you about focusing on a niche, your next step should be to find as much information about that niche as possible. To do any kind of marketing to any kind of customers you need to first *know* about your customers and connect with them. Connecting comes by knowing who, what, why, when, where and how. These are the 6 connection questions that Gary Keller talks about in his book "Shift".

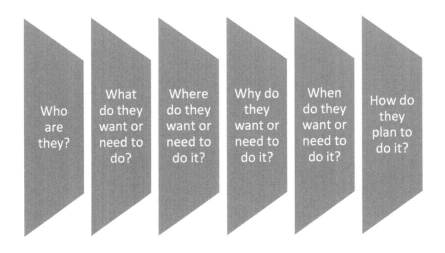

Luckily, if you research enough there is lot of information available. NAR research does an awesome job of profiling different kind of buyers and sellers. For example, if you wanted to focus on First Time Home Buyers or Single Females this is what you can find in the "Profile of Home Buyers and Sellers 2010" published by NAR Research.

First Time Home Buyers:

- Median Household Income - $59,900
- Median Square Feet they buy – 1540
- Median Age – 30

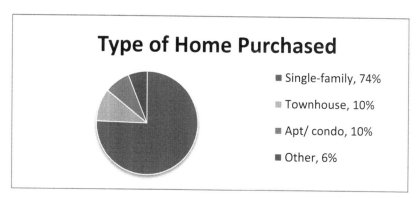

Single Females:

- Median Household Income - $50,600
- Median Square Feet they buy – 1450
- Median Age – 41

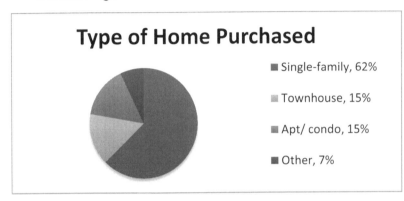

Type of Home Purchased

- Single-family, 62%
- Townhouse, 15%
- Apt/ condo, 15%
- Other, 7%

Reasons to Purchase Home

- Desire to own, 39%
- Tax credit, 11%
- Family changes, 10%
- Affordability, 6%

How Buyer Purchased Home

- Agent, 82%
- Builder, 6%
- Previous Owner, 6%
- Foreclosure, 5%

Suggested reading on Niche Marketing – "The Long Tail" by Chris Anderson

Let's get to planning now. An integral part of planning is understanding your numbers and ratios. Ask yourself these questions:

- What is my goal for next year – net commission earned?
- What is my average transaction size?
- How many transactions do I need to do to reach my commission goal?
- How many representing the buyers, how many representing the sellers?
- What is my lead to client ratio?
- How many leads do I need for the year to reach my goal, how many for the month, how many for the week?

Once you have these numbers figured out, it's much easier to plan.

While lead generation or prospecting should always take priority in planning, don't fail to plan for the other 2 stages of your business. Investing time and energy into converting leads and remaining in touch after the close will more likely double your business compared to the situation where your sole focus is generating new leads.

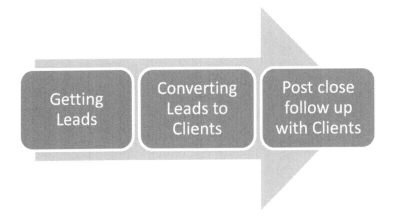

Getting Leads: There are several ways in which you can generate leads.

- Calls to your sphere of influence
- Agent referrals
- Open Houses
- Expired Listings
- Client Parties
- Online and Social Media Marketing
- FSBO's
- Direct Mail campaigns
- Newspaper, magazine and cable television advertising and marketing
- Promotional items like calendars, magnets, and personal license plates

- Signs and brochure boxes
- Sponsorships

What we would like to talk about is creating several pillars for your lead generation. If you are currently getting most of your leads only from one source e.g. SOI (Sphere of Influence), you need to look at other channels too. Look at creating 4-5 solid pillars for generating leads. If you would like to explore some of the ways to generate leads beyond traditional ways, try these:

Open Houses beyond the basics

1. Yard Signs with balloons and rider
2. Yard Signs with directions
3. Flyers the week before to neighbors for an exclusive weeknight open house, e-mail invites to database
4. Extend neighborhood reach to another 100 neighbors with e-mail invites and then call the morning of open house to remind them
5. Set up an information resource center in the open house with information on the property but other information like mortgage information and requirements for this specific property, statistics on neighborhood recent sales, information on schools in the area, information on property taxes, how to hold

title etc… anything that people will stop by and pick up

Do this and your open house will be beyond basic it will stand out from the crowd and be a reason for a visitor to come and find you first to get the information thus enabling you a chance to talk to them.

Networking – Organizations like BNI, LeTip and Meetup could be great referral sources. You can also network with other local business owners by joining your Chamber of Commerce. The trick with joining any networking group is that you should be ready to take one of the leadership positions to get more visibility.

Online Marketing – This is now more a necessity than an option. This *has* to be one of your pillars for lead generation. Read the chapter on "Generating business on the web" earlier in this book.

Leverage your Lender – You can partner up with your lender to create all sort of co-branded marketing events like Home Buyer Seminars, Avoid Foreclosure Seminars,

Investor Seminar, Special financing like FHA Rehab program or Short-Sale Seminars. Note these events can also be delivered online via webinars. You can also work with your lender partner to work with FSBOs. When FSBOs are contacted directly by a real estate agent they are more guarded and circumspect. However if you can find the leads (via Craigslist for free or a paid Landvoice subscription), get your lender to establish the initial contact, FSBOs could be more open to talk. Lender could offer pre-qualification, marketing of property via single property websites, blogs and other social media platform etc. to offer value to the FSBOs. But if they are not able to sell it on their own and ready to hire an agent, the lender would be able to connect you with them. Try it for few months and see how it works.

Converting Leads to Clients: Has it ever happened to you? You meet someone at a networking event or get a lead from your website who mentions that he would like to buy a house in some future time but not right now. And you let that contact go.

It's said that most important asset in the real estate business is your database; and by that I don't only mean your closed clients but also active and inactive leads who could potentially become your clients in the future. Remember – *every contact is a lead*. The person who nurtures that contact/lead in the best possible way wins.

If you constantly provide something of value, when they do make a decision to buy, you will be the first person they will think of. While contacts in person and via mail are important too, you can achieve this fairly inexpensive by email marketing. Read the chapter on "Generating business on the web" for more details.

Remaining in touch with your past clients: In a recent survey conducted by NAR, 88% of the home buyers who used a Real Estate agent mentioned that they were very satisfied. 66% said that they would definitely recommend the same agent and 22% said they would probably recommend the same agent. But in reality, less than 20% end up using the same agent for their next transaction. So looks like given an opportunity, agents do a great job of providing the knowledge and service required, but they do a terrible job of following up with their clients once a transaction closes.

By improving your follow up systems, you can not only ensure that your clients use you for their next transaction they will also refer you to their friends and family. Sounds simple, but as the data suggests most of the agents either do it on an *ad hoc* basis or worse don't do it at all.

A research suggested that you need to "touch" a client 22 times a year to remain on top of their mind. Before you have an OMG moment, let us tell you that it's not as difficult as it sounds. There are at least 4 different ways in which you can remain in touch with your clients (as illustrated in the picture below). Note that a combination of all 4 mediums almost always work better than just 1 or 2 alone.

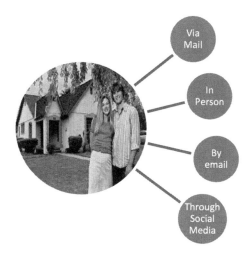

What are the different things you can do to remain in touch?

- Annual Client Appreciation party
- Holiday cards

- Birthday and Anniversary Cards
- Real Estate Trends stats for their neighborhood
- Monthly Newsletter
- Education events for home owners
- Regular rate update to inform them of an opportunity to Refinance (partner with your lender on this)

As you can see if you combine all 4 mediums and some of the ideas mentioned above, it's not that difficult to implement a 22 touch per year program.

Invest in a top quality Customer Relationship Management (CRM) tool to keep a track of all your leads and clients. Some of the popular CRM tools are:

- Act for Real Estate http://www.act.com/products/act-industry-solutions/#fragment-3
- SalesForce for Small Business http://www.salesforce.com/smallbusinesscenter/
- Top Producer http://www.topproducer.com/

Execute - "The fundamental qualities for good *execution* of a plan is first; intelligence; then discernment and judgment, which enable one to recognize the best method as to attain it; the singleness of purpose; and, lastly, what is most essential of all, will-stubborn will." - *Marshall Ferdinand, Commander in chief of the Allied armies in World War I*

Even the best laid plans are only worth the paper they are written on, unless implemented. Profitable results in your business are a reflection of the action that you take. You can read several books or attend several seminars on this topic. But execution is simply a 2 step process.

Step 1 - Create Your Must Work Week!

Based on your tasks and your goals, formulate a "must work week" schedule. Arrange your day and insert - prior to it happening- your work week. At what time will you do admin related work? What days will you schedule appointments? At what time will you "prospect?" Attach those tasks on those days and times, numeric goals to coincide with your weekly numbers derived from your planning exercise.

Time blocking is a simple yet probably the most effective tool to stick to your plan. If you had planned to prospect 3 hours every day (which you should), avoid your cell phones and emails during that time. Time blocking for prospecting should always be planned at the beginning of the day before other "stuff" gets in the way.

Step 2 - Commit to Your Must Work Week!

Treat this "must work week" as if it is your sacred Bible. Put it up on a "goal board" where you can see it every day. Of course, things will change and flexibility will be required, but commit to sticking to it as much as possible. Ask yourself this question when you ever consider altering your schedule, "If you were sitting across from a customer who was handing you a check for business, would you leave the meeting to answer a phone call, would you jump on e-mail, or would you check your voice mail?" If the answer is no, then it's not an emergency.

Stay the path. And if you are struggling to stay the path make someone hold you accountable – your colleague or a family member. Try these productivity tips:

- Check your emails and voice mails only twice during the day.
- Get the most important tasks done before 11:00 am.
- Do not scatter your meetings across days, times and geography. Decide the agenda and the end time even before you get into the meeting.
- Try these amazing online tools to save several hours every week:

Last Pass – It's a password manager that remembers all your logins and password and makes web browsing easier and more secure. www.LastPass.com

Evernote – With Evernote you can capture anything, your ideas, things you hear, things you see, web site addresses of important stuff or just your notes. And you can access it anywhere. It works with nearly every computer, phone and mobile device. www.Evernote.com

Drop Box – *Dropbox* is the easiest way to store, sync, and, share files online. Access it on your computer, iPad or smart phone. www.DropBox.com

DocuSign – Get all your documents signed electronically. DocuSign is a complete web-based eSign solution. It's simple, convenient and legally binding. DocuSign works with iPhone, iPad, Android phones and of course almost all kinds of computers. http://www.docusign.com/docusign-for-real-estate/product

To get some more tips on how you can improve your productivity, download this ebook for free – "Your best just got better – 7 Keys to a more productive day" by Jason Womack.

http://www.allaboutnews.com/unl_content/eBook_The_Best.pdf

If nothing seems to work, try hiring a coach. Best coaches not only guide you in formulating a business plan that fits your goal but also help you execute that plan.

Measure - "What gets measured, gets managed" – *Peter Drucker, Management Theorist, Author of 21 books, Recipient of Presidential Medal of Freedom*

Every week you should spend some time (recommended – minimum of 2 hours) working "on the business" i.e. tracking your goals, measuring your results, and creating your must work next week.

When measuring results, use Pareto's 80/20 rule. Always be looking for top 20% i.e. which 20% activities are resulting in 80% business and bottom 20% i.e. which 20% results are taking 80% of your time. It's not always 80/20; it could be 75/25 or even 90/10.

For all very high time consuming activities that are generating very little business try taking them through a 3 step filter.

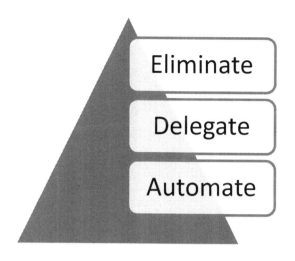

We all get used to doing our things a certain way and it becomes a habit. It requires a change of mindset to go through this process. You can use the flow-chart on the next page to be your guide when deciding.

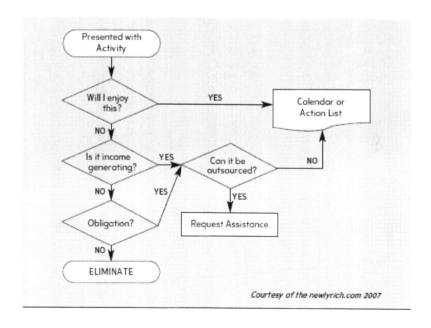

Courtesy of the newlyrich.com 2007

Eliminate – The first thing you should look for in a certain system or activity which doesn't produce direct results, is if you can eliminate it altogether. Think about that buyer who takes so much of your time but never makes an offer even when you find her exactly the place she wanted. Letting her go may be a better idea than wasting any more time.

Delegate – One of the greatest benefits of globalization of economy is outsourcing. If you do not have the budget to hire a local assistant for $3000/month, consider outsourcing some of your activities. From mundane tasks like taking your phone calls and reserving a restaurant for your client party to more complex stuff like writing blogs, managing websites and researching the web for you, a virtual assistant can do it all. Did I mention at a fraction of the price? Two of the biggest websites that have thousands of registered contractors from all over the world including USA and Canada ready to perform almost any task that you can think of are:

www.Odesk.com

www.elance.com

Recommended reading on this topic – "The World is flat" by Thomas Friedman and "4 hour work week" by Timothy Ferriss

Automate – If you can't eliminate it and can't (or don't want to) delegate it; see if you can automate it so that you can save time. There are several useful automation tools, some of which I have detailed below. If you are looking for something specific Google it and chances are you will find something that meets your requirements.

TubeMogul - If you've ever created a video and spent 3 hours posting it to many of the social video hosting websites out there then you need to take a look at this service ASAP. It's totally free to use and is a "big" time saver when it comes to getting your message out there and in front of the most number of people.

More than just automating the distribution of your videos TubeMogul will also give you countless statistics about your videos including how many people have watched them! www.TubeMogul.com

Ping.fm - What we like about Ping.fm is how much time it saves you. In fact this has got to be one of the biggest time savers out there when it comes to syndicating your content across the very best social networking websites.

The way Ping.fm works is you post your message on their website and that message gets posted to up to 40 social networking websites like Facebook, Plaxo and LinkedIn. www.ping.fm

Also try www.HootSuite.com or www.Dlvr.it

Survey Monkey - Don't let this name fool you. It's not a system for surveying monkeys. Although it's probably easy enough for a monkey to use! What Survey Monkey does is it gives you a "super" easy way of creating surveys. It's through these surveys that you can find out what your customers want and need. When you know those answers marketing becomes a whole lot easier!
www.SurveyMonkey.com

Mind Jet Manager - This will help you to shortcut the process of coming up with ideas. We are sure you've heard of mind mapping before, well this software takes it to the next level whenever you need to brainstorm a new idea or develop new systems and procedures for the streamlining your online business. www.MindJet.com

IGetSales - Set specific and measurable goals using the business planning module. Your progress toward your key business metrics is then tracked for you automatically. You'll know the instant that a "course correction" is needed.

Focus on the few key activities that truly drive real estate sales. You'll know exactly how much of each activity you need to engage in to reach the goals you've set for yourself. http://igetsales.net/.

THE CONSTITUTION OF SUCCESS

"There are no short cuts to any place worth going" - Beverly Sills

There is a constitution for success and it is important because it gives you a road map for how to get there. Use it.

- Aim beyond what you are capable of
- Realize that nothing is impossible
- Accept that there are no excuses
- Don't promise what you cannot deliver
- If you are stuck go a new way
- Don't take no for an answer
- When it cannot be done do it anyway
- Don't be afraid of your silly ideas
- Don't be afraid to work with the best
- Fail better next time
- Seek criticism
- Don't look for the next opportunity look for the one you already have.

- Remember it's not only what you know but also who know you
- Without having a goal it's difficult to score

So knowing that real estate is a cyclical business with up and down cycles these moments of chaos are opportunities. First, you need to double your efforts to grow your business—not double your time but doubling of your focus and intensity so that you are more effective and efficient.

Embrace Opportunity

By embracing the opportunities of what is out there traditional and new in marketing and branding you will be more successful. As Winston Churchill said winning starts with beginning and here are the things to focus on as you begin:

- Look at what you do best and do more of it.
- Run your business like a real business. Invest in it don't just spend money. Build your revenues don't just wait for the phone to ring.
- Understand lead generation and that it is your job 1—an everyday thing. Each day you must seek out new leads.

- Make the Internet your friend as it's too important a marketing/branding tool to ignore.
- Participate in the markets that will be active—that means that for the next few years both the traditional markets but also the foreclosure and short sale markets.
- Build a team of valuable partners including lenders, escrow officers etc. as getting a transaction to fund and close is harder than ever. Remember a team is always stronger than an individual.
- Get educated and stay current on the economy and real estate and how they interconnect, what markets are hot and which are not and why, understand value versus valuation, who controls the market etc.
- Know what your job is—it's not just to sell and list real estate. Today it is to create real estate opportunities, minimize risks and show your clients how they can build ongoing wealth through real estate.

No one said it would be easy or should be easy. What you do is who you become. Plans, actions, results not easy but pretty clear-cut when you think about it. Know your goals and where you currently stand. Then know where you want to go and if something is stopping you from getting there.

We all seem to start great out of the gate but success belongs to those who finish. Thus, success comes to those who chose it.

Now it's your turn to choose—what will it be?

BIBLIOGRAPHY

1. National Association of Realtors
2. Emerging Trends in Real Estate 2011 - PricewaterhouseCoopers
3. The State of the Nation's Housing 2010, The Joint Center for Housing Studies of Harvard University
4. US Census Bureau
5. TransUnion
6. Urban Land Institute
7. Freddie Mac
8. HUD.gov
9. Zillow.com

7950778R0

Made in the USA
Charleston, SC
24 April 2011